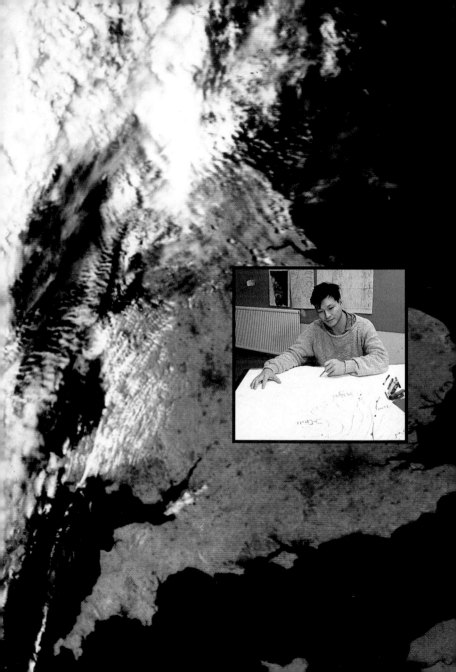

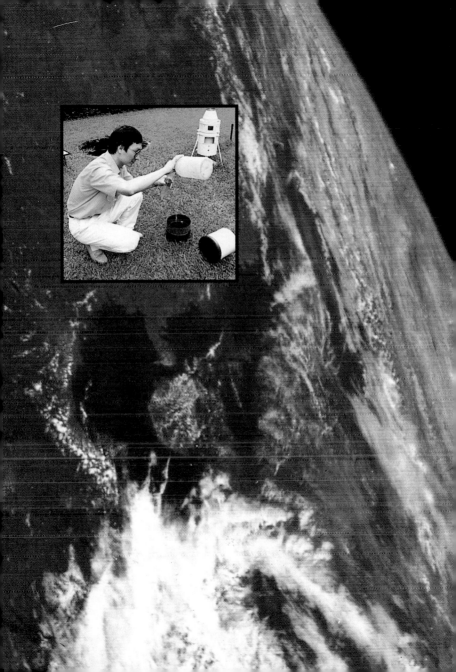

CONTENTS

WEATHER
DRAMA OF THE HEAVENS

René Chaboud

DISCOVERIES

HARRY N. ABRAMS, INC., PUBLISHERS

Ever mindful that their very lives depend on the weather, human beings have left no avenue unexplored in their efforts to predict it. They have scanned the skies, observed celestial bodies, studied the behavior of animals, prayed to the Almighty, and cursed the devil. But the answer to that deceptively simple question—what will tomorrow's weather be?—did not begin to emerge until the age of scientific research was well under way.

CHAPTER I
IN THE BEGINNING
THERE WAS THE SKY

Ancient mythology, the book of Genesis, and folklore all attest to the age-old impulse to endow heavenly bodies and celestial phenomena with human characteristics. Anthropomorphism extended not just to the sun and moon (right, a 19th-century French cartoon) but to the Almighty, shown here separating light from darkness in a 15th-century bible (opposite).

M. le *Soleil* et Mme la *Lune* ayant appris un matin que leur cousine la *Terre* est bien mal, projettent ensemble de

During the coldest part of the last glacial period, eighteen thousand years ago, the sea level was four hundred feet lower than it is today: One could walk dryshod from France to England. But 120,000 years ago, when the Earth was in the midst of a "warm spell," the sea level was about twenty feet higher, and vast expanses of the globe were under water. Adaptive, resourceful human beings bore up under these tremendous changes in climate and continued to thrive. Our population growth lends ever-increasing urgency to the question of the climate's future. What if our fragile, polluted atmosphere were suddenly to leave us with an environment no longer fit for human life? That prospect alone should stimulate interest in meteorology, the science of the atmosphere and its phenomena.

Our Quest to Understand and Predict the Weather Reaches Back to the Stone Age

Our sharp-eyed, surefooted forebears were skilled hunters. Wind direction, the appearance of the sky, the amount of moisture in the air, and tracks in the snow provided valuable

One theory is that cataclysmic floods led to the mass extinction of the dinosaurs during the Late Cretaceous period (above).

information about their quarry's movements. When they settled down and began to cultivate crops, it became increasingly clear that practical knowledge of weather phenomena could spell the difference between life and death.

Signs possibly representing the sun and rain, or the sun and moon with halos around them, appear in rock paintings found in Scotland dating from between 12,000 and 6000 BC. Although early weather forecasting was little more than divination, it is known to have assumed a prominent place in human culture by the time writing evolved. Inscribed terra-cotta tablets from the 12th century BC reveal that the ancient Babylonians worked out a system for classifying and interpreting climate-related events. One such inscription forever prophesies: "When a halo surrounds the sun, rain will fall. When a cloud grows dark in the sky, the wind will blow."

Further evidence of weather's long-standing importance to humankind can be found in the book of Genesis, which chronicles the most cataclysmic meteorological event of all time: the Flood. Even allowing for overstatement on the part of biblical narrators—Noah was said to be six hundred years old when God's punishment began—the fact remains that torrential downpours and raging storms could arouse dread, inspire awe, and command respect in puny earthbound humans.

The characters inscribed on this piece of tortoiseshell from between 1339 and 1281 BC (below) indicate that the Chinese kept weather records for ten-day periods at least as far back as the 14th century BC. Part of the inscription reads: "Third day, rain during the night; fifth day, rain early in the morning; sixth day, rain and wind in the evening; tenth day, strong wind from the north."

Babylonian astronomer-priests practicing under the auspices of their chief deity, Marduk, were among the first to work out meteorological rules of thumb, if not systematic forecasts. This kudurru, a Babylonian field boundary stone (opposite below), depicts various celestial bodies.

Weather and the Philosophers of Antiquity

Until it is proven otherwise, the Chinese are credited with the first regular weather observations. Inscriptions from the Shang dynasty (1766–1122 BC) describe sky conditions, snow height, and wind characteristics for ten consecutive days. Official record-keeping of climate-related phenomena was initiated in 1066 BC.

In around 600 BC in pre-Socratic Greece, Thales of Miletus (625?–547? BC) devised the first weather calendar for sailors. And this weather-wise natural philosopher was not above putting his expertise to shrewder use. Legend has it that just before a drought he purchased a bountiful crop of olives, cornered the market, and made a killing!

In his wide-ranging *Meteorologica*, Aristotle (384–322 BC) commented not only on such subjects as clouds, rain, dew, snow, hail, and storms, but also on rainbows, halos, and other atmospheric optical phenomena. Aristotle's undeniable inaccuracies should not overshadow his impressive grasp of water condensation: The difference between rain, dew, snow, and frost, he argued, is attributable to cooling in varying degrees. Expanded by his disciple Theophrastus (c. 372–c. 287 BC), who himself published a treatise on winds, Aristotle's comprehensive discussion was considered the authority on weather theory for over two thousand years.

Of Frogs and Romans

Frogs entered Western weather lore around 278 BC, when the Greek physician and poet Aratus, best remembered for his didactic poem on astronomy, *Phaenomena*, wrote, "If croaking frogs drone in the swamps, drenching rain shall fall from the clouds." Some Greek scholars ventured actual predictions, virtually all of which were

Unlike the Babylonians and Chaldeans, who believed that atmospheric phenomena depended solely on the movement of the stars, Greek philosopher Anaxagoras of Miletus (c. 500–428 BC, left) sought to fathom the laws governing the atmosphere, especially cloud formation and the relationship between altitude and air temperature.

The moon was of overriding importance to Thales (above), as it had been to the Babylonians and Chaldeans. He is said to have predicted the solar eclipse of 585 BC.

"The reflection of the sun in the clouds is called a rainbow. It is a sign of stormy weather, for the water that permeates the clouds produces wind or rain."

Anaxagoras

based on interpretations of the aspect and movement of celestial bodies.

In ancient Rome, the great poet Virgil (70–19 BC) let the sun, the moon, and animal behavior be his guides and recorded his observations in the first book of his pastoral poem, the *Georgics*: "Rain never need surprise us unprepared, for when it rises, airborne cranes take off

Lightning and waterspouts (13th-century manuscript, above) are among the phenomena Roman poet Lucretius (c. 95–c. 54 BC) discusses in *De Rerum Natura*.

and glide along the valley floor." According to Roman scholar Pliny the Elder (AD 23–79), "A red moon is a sign of wind, a black moon a sign of rain."

Meanwhile, on the other side of the Alps, Goths and Gauls shot arrows at advancing storm clouds to keep the sky from crashing down on them.

God, the Devil, and the Elements

Given the remarkable strides made under the impetus of Greek and Roman philosophers and poets, the science of meteorology seemed destined for a fine future. Unfortunately, however, it sunk into oblivion. Caught up in a never-ending cycle of warfare, people turned instead to the supernatural as a quick fix for whatever bedeviled them. During the Middle Ages, speculation about weather and the elements was lumped together with astrology and classed among the occult sciences, resulting in a long obscurantist period devoid of probing inquiry.

French chroniclers occasionally reported weather events but made no attempt to explain them. We know, for example, that December 1302 was extraordinarily cold, because "people were found frozen to death in their beds."

SAINT DONAT, MARTYR.

In 1557, the year this woodcut was made (above), people believed that raindrops fell simply because the Almighty willed it so. God in his infinite power could just as easily ordain a shower of crosses.

Miraculous survivor of a lightning strike, Saint Donatus (left) was widely believed to provide protection from lightning. Traditionally depicted in Roman armor and bearing both a sword and the martyr's palm, he alone had the power to fend off the celestial fire.

Commenting on the harsh winter of the famine years of 1315–6 one author noted in his history of England that "utmost care had to be taken to hide children from view lest they be snatched by starving thieves." Manuscripts from the time are full of revealing anecdotes:

The assumption that God's mighty hand ruled the heavens (*Deus Regit Astra*, left) meant that all celestial phenomena were interpretable signs that allowed humans to divine their Creator's purpose. For centuries, shooting stars were believed to be long-range weather predictors; more of them than usual foretold a severe winter. A comet streaking across the sky was a decidedly bad omen that presaged both strong wind and drought.

"During the summer of 1282, poor people in Alsace were eating new wheat two weeks before St. John's Day [24 June] and pumpkins by St. Margaret's Day [20 July]. The grape harvest took place before Saint Croix's Day [14 September]." But around the year 1000, some perceptive soul had deduced that "east-borne frost is not soon lost," thus making a connection between cold air masses from Siberia and persistent frost—quite an accomplishment for the time! As far as most people were concerned, however, God alone had the power to bring about changes in the weather. In time of drought they offered up countless prayers for rain, and in time of flood prayed no less fervently for the rain to stop. When their prayers went unanswered, they blamed the devil and his evil ways.

"Great Saint Donatus, pray for me.
May no storms around me blow,
May kin and friend be spared their woe.
May they rage far out at sea,
Where no boats or vessels be."
Prayer to Saint Donatus

The Common Sense of Folk Sayings

In the 16th century, proverbs and sayings took over where "divine meteorology" had left off. Based on accumulated observations and inferences and usually devised by country folk, these pithy nuggets of weather wisdom were passed on by word of

Grâce aux tendres soins de M. *Soleil* et de Mme la *Lune* ses parents, Mme la *Terre* est bientôt rétablie, et donne le

mouth and then from almanac to almanac. Their popularity had as much to do with the humor of their form as with the reliability of their content. The most felicitous sayings managed to combine usefulness and wit: "A mackerel sky and a berouged lover—one's as short-lived as the other." But others—such as "Christmas on the balcony, Easter by the fireside" or "On the eve of Candlemas Day [7 February], the winter gets stronger or passes away"—seem to have caught on primarily because of a droll rhyme or clever twist.

Those weather proverbs rooted in careful observation had some real meteorological value. Many are surprisingly perceptive and prove their worth to this day: "The farther the sight, the nearer the rain" or "A ring around the sun or moon, means that rain is coming soon."

The popularity of homespun sayings was at its peak in France when the English shed some of their already legendary impassivity and passed a law in 1677 declaring

The underlying objective of the childlike world depicted in these French prints, an early form of comic strip, was to instill sound values in the minds of young readers (left and below). The action-filled episodes portray Mr. Sun, Mrs. Moon, Miss Rain, Papa Thunder, Miss Hail, Mr. Wind, and Mrs. Snow as members of a family, which if nothing else conveyed the idea that the components of the atmosphere are interdependent. Although unquestionably unscientific, the cartoons strive to set an educational tone best summed up in the concluding moral: "The Sun, my dears, is the Creator's eye; without it flower, beast, and man would die."

En se laissant rouler du sommet de montagnes, Mme la *Neige* anéantit sou elle l'habitant du vallon.

De son côté papa *Tonnerre*, vieux et rusé coquin, tuait et incendiait ce qu'il trouvait en route.

Mlle la *Grêle* et compère *Ouragan* détruisent toutes les moissons des enfants de Mme la *Terre*.

La Lune Rousse

Gardeners once thought the dreaded red moon (left) froze the young shoots they would find irreparably blighted on spring mornings. Since such damage seemed to occur only when the moon shone brightly overhead, popular tradition blamed its light. French physicist François Arago (1786–1853) investigated the phenomenon and showed that frost is most apt to be formed when there is no cloud cover to keep the Earth's warmth from radiating away. And when there is no cloud cover, of course, the moon appears. Radiational cooling, not the moon or its light, was the culprit.

"Clear moon,
Frost soon."
Popular saying

that all "rainmakers and weather seers" would be burned at the stake. This measure was pointedly ignored, relegated to oblivion, and upon its rediscovery finally repealed—in 1959!

M. le *Vent* était partout ! ici frappant les flancs de la mer, il la met en furie et fait sombrer le nautonnier.

Là, de concert avec Mlle la *Pluie* sa sœur, ils ouvrent les réservoirs des cieux, et les enfants de Mme la *Terre* meurent tous par le déluge.

MORALITÉ.

Le Soleil, mes enfants, c'est l'œil du Créateur Vivifiant lui seul, homme, animal ou fleur.

The Advent of Scientific Instruments

While empirical folk wisdom was busy crafting quaint
rhyming predictions, scientists were gradually forging
their own principles and perfecting weather instruments.

The late 17th and
early 18th centuries
witnessed a spate of
scientific discoveries.
In 1643 Evangelista
Torricelli demonstrated
the existence of air
pressure and invented
the barometer to
measure it. Europeans
were using rain gauges
as far back as 1639. The
hygrometer, which
measures atmospheric
humidity, was invented
in 1664. The earliest
anemometers date from
1667; these instruments
measure wind speed.
Improved thermometers
were in use by 1730.

About 1765 French scientist Antoine Lavoisier
(1743–94) proposed the first practical guidelines for
weather prediction: "The prediction of prospective
changes in the weather is an art with its own rules and
procedures and requires the wide-ranging experience
of a seasoned physicist. The following will be needed:
routine daily observation of fluctuations in the
height of the mercury in a barometer, the strength
and direction of the wind at various elevations, the
moisture content of the air.... With all this information, it is almost always possible to predict the weather
for one or two days ahead with reasonable accuracy.
This would, in our view, be very useful to society."

The laws of physics that describe the behavior of
a gas under various conditions of pressure, volume,
and temperature were formulated by the early 19th
century, setting the stage for a deeper understanding

of the dynamics of atmospheric phenomena. Governments began to realize that this expanding body of knowledge might have practical applications worth investigating.

A Tactician's Friend—or Foe

Weather conditions are known to have figured decisively in some of the ruthless wars that punctuate ancient history. During his 56–54 BC campaign against the Veneti, a Celtic people of ancient Gaul, Julius Caesar was confronted by storms that demolished a good many of his ships, first off the coast of Brittany and subsequently in the English Channel. When Kublai Khan, Genghis Khan's grandson and founder of the Mongol dynasty, sent a naval expedition to conquer Japan in 1274, his army of 35,000 men and fleet of seven hundred ships were overwhelmed by a ferocious typhoon; more than a third of his men were killed. In 1281 he tried again with a combined invading force of 140,000 Mongols, Koreans, and Chinese. Another

French scientists Joseph Louis Gay-Lussac and Jean-Baptiste Biot made a scientific balloon ascent in 1804 (above) thanks to a fundamental law of atmospheric dynamics: Heated air rises because it is lighter than the colder air around it.

Opposite. In 1777 French chemist and physicist Antoine Lavoisier concluded that air is composed of oxygen and "non-respirable air," later renamed nitrogen. His estimate of the relative volume of oxygen (27%) is fairly close to the actual figure (21%).

Left: Even simulated, phenomena such as lightning could prove unexpectedly powerful, as the Russian physicist Georg Wilhelm Richmann demonstrated on 6 August 1753 when an electrical experiment he was performing in St. Petersburg cost him his life.

EVANGELISTA TORRICELLI

1

2

A C B

3

4

The Hygrometer

Measuring the moisture content of air, or humidity, did not begin until the 18th century. (1) The first true mechanical hygrometer, built around 1780 by Swiss physicist and geologist Horace Bénédict de Saussure, used ordinary human hair, which stretches as it absorbs moisture. (3) One type of balance hygrometer used cotton as an absorbing substance. (4) This glass balance hygrometer was made in the 17th century.

The Barometer

In 1643, Italian scientist Evangelista Torricelli (2) demonstrated that the pressure air exerts on the Earth's surface supports a column of mercury 29.92 inches (76 centimeters) in height. (6) All barometers can be traced back to his experiment, which Blaise Pascal and Robert Boyle (5) repeated elsewhere in 1648 and 1661, respectively.

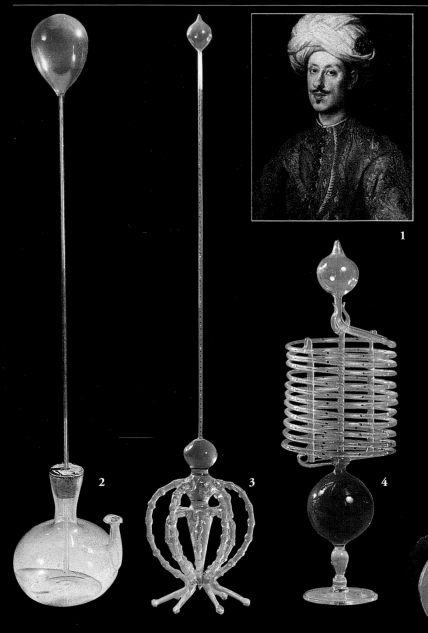

2

3

4

1

The Thermometer

The first sealed liquid-in-glass air thermometer, although developed in 1641 at the court of Grand Duke Ferdinand II of Tuscany (1), here dressed as a Turk, was based on principles Galileo had set forth in 1597. The issue of stem calibration was hotly debated because there was no standard for marking graduated scales. Finally, in 1694, Carlo Renaldini, a physicist from Padua, proposed that the freezing and boiling points of water be used as fixed points in thermometric scales. Then, in 1714, German physicist Daniel Fahrenheit invented his namesake thermometer and was the first to use mercury to measure temperature. Sixteen years later René de Réaumur devised another system, and in 1742 Anders Celsius introduced the centigrade scale. (2) A 19th-century reproduction of the 1597 thermoscope Galileo invented while in Padua; (3 and 4) two 1657 glass thermometers, tributes as much to the art of glassblowing as to the spirit of scientific inquiry; (5) a mercury thermometer Lavoisier used; and (6) an early Fahrenheit thermometer, with scales for Réaumur and Celsius as well.

typhoon struck, obliterating his fleet and dashing his dream of empire once and for all.

Rain proved a crucial force at a key conflict in the Hundred Years War, the Battle of Crécy (26 August 1346). English archers came equipped with protective covers for their longbows, a "minor point" Philip VI of France had overlooked. The French, armed with more powerful crossbows, were routed by the enemy's stronger, more accurate arrowshots. History repeated itself at the Battle of Agincourt on 25 October 1415. The heavily armored French, mired in a sodden field, were cut down by the more lightly equipped, more mobile English.

In 1776, during the Revolutionary War, George Washington found his troops surrounded and mired in the mud at Valley Forge. A north wind brought lower temperatures, froze the ground, and made it possible for the American troops to escape. Another revolutionary war, this one in France, might never have come to pass if the punishing winter of 1788–9 had not come on the heels of the previous summer's crop-damaging hailstorms; the resulting famine fanned social unrest.

"My Dear Sirs"

In the wake of "climatic aberrations," the French Home Secretary issued a statement to prefects throughout the nation in 1821: "My dear sirs, as we have seen over the past few years, France seems increasingly to have fallen prey to spells of markedly cooler temperatures, unexpected variability in the seasons, and highly unusual

The hailstorms that devastated wheat crops in northern France (above) in July 1788 left famine and poverty in their wake.

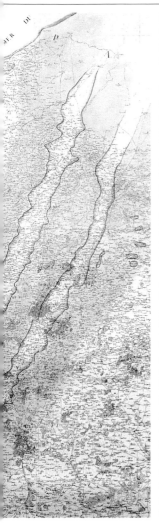

hurricanes and floods." He went on to ask the prefects to investigate these "aberrations" and report their findings.

The list of suspected culprits ranged from the deforestation of France or America to earth-quakes, volcanic eruptions, and even magnetic declination. The one exception was the prefect of Charente, who submitted a reply that was as sensible as it was terse: "The cause of these aberrations shall continue to elude us so long as the government fails to make daily weather observation compulsory."

A Gale Whips Up Interest in Meteorology

On 14 November 1854 the French warship *Henri IV* and thirty-eight merchantmen sank in a fierce storm near the port of Balaklava during the Crimean War, claiming four hundred lives. The French minister of war at the time, Marshal Vaillant, asked astronomer Urbain Leverrier (1811–77) to look into the circumstances surrounding the disaster. By showing that the "surprise" storm had already formed by 12 November and then swept across Europe from northwest to southeast, the noted scientist showed that weather phenomena travel across the Earth's surface. Modern meteorology had taken its first step.

Realizing that cities could exchange information and use it to locate storms and predict their movement, the

Urbain Leverrier (above), director of the Paris Observatory, is regarded as the father of modern meteorology. Citing the loss of the warship *Henri IV* in a surprise storm on 14 November 1854, during the Crimean War (opposite left), he argued that weather forecasting was in urgent need of improvement. The next year the French government recognized meteorology as "an eminently practical science, the progress of which particularly affects navigation, agriculture, public works, and hygiene."

The Second International Meteorological Congress held in Rome in April 1879 (left) recommended the formation of a nine-member committee (including the Dutch meteorologist Buys Ballot, opposite right) to "help standardize and synchronize the exchange of observations among central institutes" and circulate publications.

French government decided that a special observation network should be set up to warn of impending storms. Of the twenty-four observing stations that made up the original 1855 meteorological network, thirteen were linked by telegraph. That was just the beginning. Other European countries were developing national weather services, and agreements of mutual cooperation paved the way for an ever-increasing flow of data across borders. By 1865 Europe's weather observation network boasted fifty-nine stations. A U.S. government weather service was established in 1870 under the Army Signal Corps.

The growing body of observational data confirmed the presumed link between changes in the weather and barometric readings. The key to predicting the weather, it seemed, was atmospheric pressure.

Synoptic Meteorology Comes of Age

In 1857 Dutch meteorologist Christoph Buys Ballot

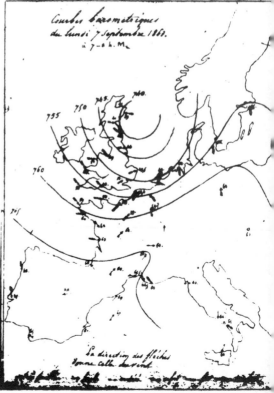

(1817–90) shed new light on the dynamics of air pressure and its influence on weather by showing that windflow always follows isobars, the lines drawn on charts to join places of equal air pressure. Barometric readings thus became the building blocks of the first-ever isobar maps, which showed pressure distribution at a given time.

The standard operating procedure developed by early synoptic meteorologists—those who used simultaneous observations made over a large area—was a model of simplicity. Step one: Plot weather observations on a map to give a general view of large-scale atmospheric conditions (extensive cloud systems, areas of rain). Step two: Infer their future movement by interpreting isobaric patterns of wind speed and direction.

Lines joining places of equal atmospheric pressure are a prominent feature of the earliest meteorological charts (below left, for western Europe, 7 and 10 September 1863). Buys Ballot showed that such isobars could be used to estimate wind speed and direction and infer cloud movement.

In 1857 Buys Ballot wrote: "Since the wind is in general perpendicular to the direction of maximum barometric slope, an easterly wind is associated with a decrease in pressure from north to south and a westerly wind with a decrease from south to north." Three years later he developed the rule of thumb that bears his name: "In the Northern Hemisphere, if you turn your back to the wind, the lower pressure will be on your left and the higher on your right."

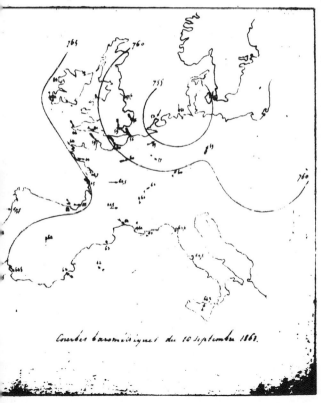

Courbes barométriques du 10 septembre 1863.

But this method had serious drawbacks. It did not take into account the impact of topography on weather and relied solely on land-based observations. The time had come to think three-dimensionally.

Weather Kites and Balloons Aloft

Clouds are steered in one direction or another by winds in the upper atmosphere. Much of the time, the characteristics of upper-air winds differ from those of winds blowing at the surface. Therefore, accurately predicting cloud movement depends on obtaining information about the upper reaches of the atmosphere.

Meteorologists used all their ingenuity to remedy the defects in the synoptic method. Léon Teisserenc de Bort (1855–1913), founder of the Observatory of Dynamic Meteorology near Paris, pioneered unmanned upper-air observation with his instrument-bearing kites and balloons; some were captive, others free-flying. But recovering the registering apparatus was at best hit or miss. Around 1930, Robert Bureau of France and Pavel Malchanov of the Soviet Union developed radiosonde observation by placing small transmitters in weather balloons so that readings could be radioed back to ground stations during ascent.

A radiosonde network evolved in the 1930s and '40s to systematically monitor and transmit data about upper-air humidity, wind, and temperature. Meanwhile, observing stations continued to proliferate. After considerable improvement, synoptic meteorology scored a number of forecasting successes, the most famous of which may have been the correct prediction for 6 June 1944, the day Allied troops landed on the coast of Normandy.

Not only did Teisserenc de Bort use anemometers and weather vanes (opposite) to study wind at the surface, but he developed sounding balloons (center) and weather kites (above) to gather information about winds aloft.

If our planet were a ball three feet in diameter, the fragile layer of air enveloping it would be a tiny fraction of an inch thick. Ninety-nine percent of the total mass of the atmosphere lies within its lowermost eighteen miles. The remaining one percent thins out with altitude and is undetectable just over nine hundred miles above the Earth's surface.

CHAPTER II
OUR RESTLESS ATMOSPHERE

Contrary to the scene depicted in this 19th-century print, no one can literally poke his head through the vaulting canopy of sky. We now know that our sun is just one of countless stars, our planet but a speck in the vastness of space, and our atmosphere nothing more than a tenuous film of gas.

The fact that many ancient religions deified the sun is a measure of how fully they understood its supreme importance. The Egyptians called their sun-god Ra or Aton, the Babylonians Shamash, the Greeks Helios or Apollo, and the Maya Kinich Ahau.

A Star We Call the Sun

We now know that the sun is but one of a hundred billion stars in our galaxy, and an unremarkable star at that. Our planet intercepts two-billionths of all available solar radiation—a trifling amount as far as the sun is concerned, but the source of all our light and heat. Were it not for that tiny bit of radiant energy, not only weather, but life as we know it would cease and the Earth's surface temperature would rise no higher than -250° C. (Editor's note: Centigrade and metric measurements, which are standardly used in scientific calculations, will be employed in this book where suitable. Please refer to page 152 for conversions.)

The sun is a fiery ball of gas 93 million miles from the Earth. Temperatures at the core of this churning cauldron can soar as high as an inconceivable 15 million degrees C, while surface temperatures range between 4000 and 6000° C. With a core pressure a hundred billion times greater than that of the Earth's atmosphere, the sun is an unimaginable thermonuclear powerhouse generating energy at a rate equal to burning 500 million tons of oil a second.

All we can do is watch and take measurements as this awesome spectacle unfolds before us. The sun continuously bathes the outer reaches of our atmosphere in radiant energy with an average value of 1370 watts/meter^2, which is called the solar constant. It is this liberally distributed energy that drives the atmosphere and the global weather. Although experts have estimated that the sun has enough fuel in reserve to sustain itself

Auroras set the night sky aglow over polar regions because the Earth's magnetic field intercepts a tiny fraction of the charged particles that solar eruptions (below) send hurtling through space.

Although in a 15th-century Italian manuscript, this representation of the sun (opposite) has a decidedly pagan, medieval look to it. A magical trilogy— the sun's heat, the lion's strength, and an allegorical figure of wisdom—forms the polar axis of a radiant disk. Meanwhile, earthbound humans do battle, compete, work, and play by its warm light.

for another few billion years, how it delivers energy
is as important as the energy itself. The workings of
our atmosphere are so heavily dependent on the sun's
behavior that even minute fluctuations in solar activity
could have an incalculable impact on our climate—
and our lives.

E Pur Si Muove!

Our planet's movement through space can be described in two all-important ways: The Earth revolves about the sun once every 365 days, and it rotates on its axis once every twenty-four hours.

"E pur si muove!" (Nevertheless it does move!): Ever since Galileo (1564–1642) muttered his statement of defiance in the face of his inquisitors—who had forced him to deny his belief that the Earth revolves around the sun— we have come to take the heliocentric view of the solar system for granted. The Earth's path of revolution is an ellipse with the sun at one of the foci. As winter approaches in the Northern Hemisphere, the Earth swings closer to the sun, reaching the point nearest it (perihelion) on 2 January. On that day, a "mere" 91 million miles separate us from the sun, and the amount of solar radiation intercepted by the Earth is at its peak. Consequently, the Earth as a whole receives more light and heat during the Northern Hemisphere's winter than it does during its summer. (It doesn't seem that way to northerners because in winter the sun's rays strike their part of the globe at an angle that spreads energy over a larger area, making it less concentrated.) The Earth and sun are farthest apart on July 5 (aphelion), when they are separated by 94 million miles.

Shaped by prevailing winds, a beech tree bears mute witness to the passing seasons: spring and fall (above), winter and summer (opposite below).

The polar axis on which the Earth rotates is tipped with respect to the plane of its elliptical orbit, making an angle of 66°34'. Since the Earth's axis is fixed in space, the way the sun's rays fall on our planet changes from one month to the next. That is what causes the change in seasons and the variable length of night and day. When the southern end of the Earth's axis is tilted toward the sun, the most direct sunlight falls on the Southern Hemisphere; it is summer there. At the same time, the Northern Hemisphere is in the grip of winter, and a six-month-long night descends on the North Pole. Half a year later, the situation is reversed. According to the astronomical calendar, the seasons begin at the solstices and equinoxes, that is, at particular points along the Earth's orbit around the sun.

In an astronomical drawing of a solar eclipse (opposite below) from *Ars Magna Lucis et Umbrae in Mundi* (1645) by German Jesuit scholar Athanasius Kircher, a black triangle with the moon as its base indicates the cone-shaped area of complete darkness. The sun looks on reassuringly as the Earth is partially darkened.

The Earth's rotation on its axis is responsible for the alternate periods of light and darkness we call day and night. Its revolution around the sun causes the seasons, as shown in an engraving of its annual orbit from Camille Flammarion's 1871 *The Atmosphere* (left).

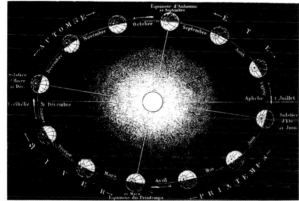

The Film of Air Around Our Planet

Air makes up nearly 98 percent of the weight of the atmosphere; water vapor and airborne particles make up the rest. Air and water are essential to all life on our planet.

Dry air is a mixture of gases with fairly constant relative volumes: nitrogen (78.09%), oxygen (20.95%), argon (0.93%), and carbon dioxide and minute traces of neon, helium, krypton, hydrogen, xenon, ozone, and radon (0.03%). The only constituents that vary by volume to any significant degree are ozone and carbon dioxide. According to many research scientists and meteorologists, these fluctuations could have far-reaching effects on global climate.

The water in the atmosphere exists in its usual three

Once the values from the wet bulb (right) and the dry bulb (left) of this Piche atmometer have been ascertained, the relative humidity of the air is calculated.

Left: The many notable achievements of Sir William Herschel (1738–1822) include his discovery of infrared radiation.

states. Water vapor—the colorless, odorless, gaseous form of water that is always in the air—is the most plentiful. Liquid water, the chief component of clouds, occurs as droplets of varying size. Only a very small amount of the water in the atmosphere is in solid form—tiny ice crystals, which are often mixed with water droplets.

Atmospheric water accounts for only a small fraction (2%) of the global stock, which is the estimated 326 million cubic miles of water contained in all of the Earth's oceans, ice sheets, glaciers, lakes, ponds, and underground reservoirs.

One last type of ingredient—microscopic solid particles of dust, volcanic ash, sand, pollen grains, sea salt, and smoke—plays a key role in the dynamics of the atmosphere.

The Spheres: Tropo, Strato, Meso, Thermo, and Exo

A thermal profile of the atmosphere reveals its two principal features: It consists of a stack of layers, and its pattern of temperature change is not uniform with increasing altitude.

Léon Teisserenc de Bort pioneered the use of weather balloons and kites to observe the upper atmosphere. In 1898 he noticed that at about six miles, the temperature not only stopped falling but rose slightly. Only after releasing hundreds of balloons to verify the seemingly incredible did he finally announce his discovery of the stratosphere, a variably high region in which temperature changes little with altitude.

The proportions of air's three main ingredients nitrogen, oxygen, and argon—are stable to an altitude of roughly fifty miles. The other atmospheric gases, however, are subject to local but significant fluctuation. For example, a forest fire can bring about a marked increase in carbon dioxide levels.

The first layer, the troposphere, extends from the surface to 4.3 miles at the poles and to about 12.5 miles

Nitrogen: 78.09%

Argon: 0.93%

Carbon dioxide and rare gases: 0.03%

Oxygen: 20.95%

at the equator, depending on the temperature. This layer is where clouds form. Generally speaking, temperature decreases with altitude throughout the troposphere at an average rate of 6.5° C per 1000 meters (about 17° F per mile). In midlatitudes, the upper boundary of the troposphere (the tropopause) varies in height from 5.5 to 7.5 miles. At this level, the temperature range is -55 to -60° C.

The next layer outward, the stratosphere, is about 18.5 miles thick. Here the temperature does a turnabout, increasing with altitude until it reaches about 0° C. This warming trend is due primarily to the presence of the ozone layer between 9 and 25 miles.

The temperature gradually drops again throughout the next layer, the mesosphere, until it reaches -120° C at an altitude of just over 50 miles, its upper boundary. In the next layer, the thermosphere, the temperature rebounds to temperatures in excess of 700° C. The exosphere starts at around 400 miles and extends for about 35 miles, thinning out and merging with the vacuum of space.

Where the Weather Is

Meteorologists rely on a number of variables to measure and evaluate atmospheric conditions, chief among them

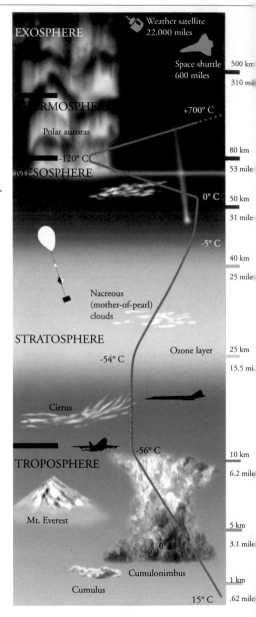

EXOSPHERE

Weather satellite
22,000 miles

Space shuttle
600 miles   500 km
                   310 mi

THERMOSPHERE   +700° C

Polar auroras

-120° C   80 km
                                53 mile

MESOSPHERE

                                0° C   50 km
                                       31 mile

                                -5° C
                                       40 km
                                       25 mile

Nacreous
(mother-of-pearl)
clouds

STRATOSPHERE

-54° C   Ozone layer   25 km
                                        15.5 mi

Cirrus

                          -56° C   10 km
                                        6.2 mile
TROPOSPHERE

Mt. Everest

                                        5 km
                                        3.1 mile

                          0° C

                          Cumulonimbus

Cumulus   1 km
                                15° C   .62 mile

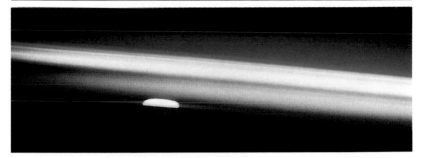

being moisture content, air pressure, and temperature.

Because our planet is in constant motion, the air surrounding it is unevenly heated by the sun. The extent to which air weighs down on the Earth's surface—that is, its pressure—changes from place to place and from one moment to the next. But if pressure were evenly distributed, the atmosphere would exert an average sea-level pressure of approximately 14.7 pounds per square inch of surface area (1.03 kg/cm²), which can be expressed in a variety of different ways: 1013 millibars or hectopascals, 29.92 inches or 760 mm of mercury. Internationally and in the scientific community, the most commonly used air pressure units are the metric millibar and kilopascal (one-tenth of a millibar), but in the United States readings are usually reported in inches of mercury.

A region where the atmospheric pressure is higher than surrounding areas is called an anticyclone or "high." A region where the atmospheric pressure is lower than surrounding areas is called a depression, cyclone, or "low." Temperature is a direct measurement of all energy transfer occurring in the atmosphere at any given time.

If the atmosphere were perfectly stable and inert, it would compliantly revolve in unison with the rotating planet beneath it. In such a world of seamless stasis, there would be no wind! But our atmosphere is anything but stable. Two factors are largely responsible for stirring things up near the surface of our planet: The sun's energy is spread very unevenly over the globe, and the world rotates.

This striking photograph of sunrise over South Africa (above) was taken from *Skylab*. The dark band between the two colored layers consists primarily of sulfuric acid droplets ejected into the stratosphere during the eruption of Mt. Pinatubo in the Philippines in 1991. This dense cloud scattered part of the sun's light toward the Earth, where it produced unusually colorful sunrises and sunsets. The rest scattered into space.

The diagram opposite illustrates the various layers of the atmosphere, which are defined by temperature. The orange line shows the change in temperature as a function of height.

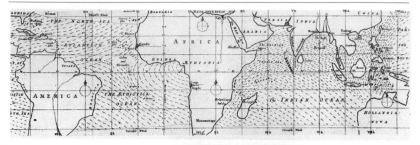

Air Conditioning on a Global Scale

Think of the imbalances in the amount of radiant energy the Earth takes in and puts out as a kind of budget. Tropical regions absorb more heat than they shed, resulting in a net surplus. The situation is reversed in polar regions, which shed more heat than they absorb. But unchecked overheating at latitudes where the sun's energy is most concentrated cannot continue indefinitely, just as accumulating energy deficits would translate into lower and lower temperatures at polar latitudes.

One way or another, things have to balance out. There has to be a mechanism that allows excess heat to be carried away from the equator toward the poles. Water is particularly capable of bringing about such transfers of energy, and we cannot underestimate the influence of ocean currents on global weather, but their role is not as critical (or, at any rate, as dynamic) as that played by the ocean of air we call the atmosphere.

If the Earth stood still, global wind patterns would be governed by the overturning motion known as convection currents. Air heated in the tropics would rise and flow aloft toward polar regions where, turning cold and dense, it would sink and begin its return trip toward the equator to replace the rising warmer air. In such a single-cell scenario, winds would continually

In 1686, English astronomer Edmond Halley (left) published the first map showing the general circulation of the winds (above). He noted that changes in the wind were directly linked to changes in barometric pressure, but he did not understand why. Halley's theory that cooler air flows in to replace rising warm air, thereby creating wind, was bold for its time.

Midlatitude cells

Tropical Hadley cells

Midlatitude cells

blow north and south from the poles to the equator. The weather in the so-called temperate latitudes would be perpetually cool, penetratingly damp, and unrelievedly overcast.

But Something Happens Between the Poles and the Equator

In 1735 George Hadley (1685–1768), an English scientist, was one of the first to picture convection on a global scale. By factoring in the Earth's rotation, he showed that warm tropical air actually sinks back toward the surface before reaching the poles; this causes the trade winds to blow. Therefore, more than one circulation loop (or "cell") was involved.

The so-called tropical Hadley cells are relatively easy to describe. Warm air rising in the tropics flows away at high altitude toward the poles. But it cools down rapidly along the way. Once cooler, and thus heavier than the surrounding air, it subsides

George Hadley argued that the circulation of the winds could be explained by a very simple system. Published in 1735, his diagram (below) shows meridional airflow. His overall concept of rising air over the tropics and sinking air over the poles proved correct, as far as it went.

Polar Hadley cells

Polar easterlies

Polar front

Prevailing westerlies

Horse latitudes

Northeast trade winds

Doldrums

Southeast trade winds

Horse latitudes

Prevailing westerlies

Polar front

Polar easterlies

Polar Hadley cells

As meteorologists filled in the gaps in Hadley's system, a more realistic, and far more complex, picture of upper-atmosphere wind circulation emerged (left).

before reaching the polar regions and flows back to the equator at low levels.

A similar process takes place at the poles. Cold, heavy air flows away at low levels toward areas of additional heat. It gradually warms up as it comes in contact with the ocean surface—and then rises and changes directions, completing a second cycle known as the polar Hadley cells.

To round out the global wind circulation picture, American meteorologist William Ferrel (1817–91) proposed a third, midlatitude segment that reversed the airflow in the Hadley cell. A few years later, in 1888, the German scientist Hermann von Helmholtz (1821–94) worked out a particularly realistic explanation of this meridional heat transfer.

The subtropical jet stream over the Red Sea and Nile River valley (above) shows up in this space photograph as a long, slender band of white. This cloud belt marks the northern limit of warm tropical air. To save on fuel, pilots ride the extremely powerful tail wind within jet streams whenever they can.

Spinning Complicates Everything

While the fact that the Earth rotates does not invalidate the heat redistribution pattern Hadley and Ferrel devised, it does add an unexpectedly dynamic wrinkle that modifies their schemes.

In a narrow zone straddling the equator, the process unfolds as predicted. Intense heating causes warm, humid air to rise, encouraging the formation of the globe-girdling "doldrums," the thunderstorm belt that shows up so dramatically on satellite photos today. But once warm tropical air starts its journey poleward, things get quite a bit more complicated. Winds blowing northward or southward from the equator do not in fact move along a straight line, because the Earth, spinning west to east at a rate of 1035 miles/hour at the equator, deflects them from their initial course. The tropical Hadley cells— the ones nearest the equator—have no alternative but to swerve: The southbound wind is turned to its right and the northbound wind to its left, creating the northeast and southeast trade winds, respectively.

Why Jet Streams Form

The closer moving air gets to the poles, the faster it blows around the polar axis. To understand why this acceleration occurs, picture an ice skater spinning slowly and gracefully with arms extended. When he pulls in his arms and aligns them with his body—his axis of rotation—his rate of spin increases and he whirls around like a top. Upper-air winds at about 30° latitude accelerate to speeds of 280 miles/hour or higher for the same reason. These incredibly fast-moving, meandering rivers of air, known as jet streams,

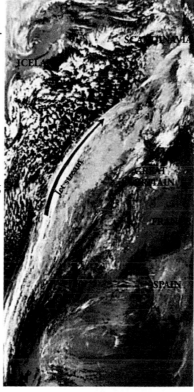

SCANDINAVIA

ICELAND

Jet Stream

GREAT BRITAIN

SPAIN

Warm tropical air flowing poleward along the Earth's curving surface speeds up the closer it gets to the axis of rotation, like a spinning ice skater with arms drawn in (left). Discovered by American fighter pilots, jet streams (above, in western Europe) play a vital part in the formation of low-pressure systems. They can swerve north and south, forming large undulations.

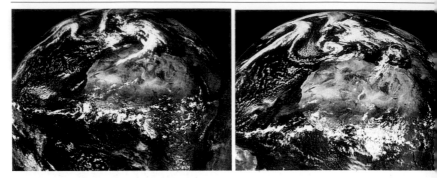

blow so powerfully they become impassable barriers that prevent warm air from continuing on its poleward journey. If nothing came along to break through these roadblocks, this is as far as tropical air would ever get. Jet streams blow roughly west to east.

Several thousand miles long but only a few high, a jet stream looks

Cold air

Warm air

1

2

Upper-Air Disturbances Spawn Lows

Meanwhile, the sun is steadily beating down on tropical regions. The ever-increasing buildup of heat keeps pumping energy into the process. Warm tropical air strains northward and southward at all costs. The upper-level airflow becomes increasingly unstable, eventually generating disturbances comparable to the swirling currents in a fast-moving river. What start out as little vortices of air gather strength, grow to variable size, and give rise to areas of low pressure, or depressions. Since the same kind of cyclonic motion can be induced by unusually high mountain ranges, the Himalayas and the Rockies are constantly susceptible to low pressure formation.

Lows can be thought of as energy transfer zones where

like a flattened tube. Jet streams can flow at between 23,000 and 33,000 feet in mid-latitudes and 33,000 to 43,000 feet in tropical regions. Violent winds generated by strong temperature contrasts blow within the tube, resulting in turbulence that encourages characteristic cloud buildup. As a disturbance gathers strength, a warm-air low-pressure core forms, "deepens," and develops into a full-blown cyclone (low-pressure frontal system) with clouds.

tropical and polar air meet. In the Northern Hemisphere, warm air from the south is pulled northward; cold air from the north is funneled toward the tropics. Were it not for these eddies in the global winds, neither air mass would get past the jet-stream barrier. In other words, lows perform the vitally important task of redistributing heat between tropical and polar regions. They keep our atmosphere's heat budget balanced.

How jet streams induce the formation of lows: Cold air surges in under a low-pressure core (1–4). Then the cold front overtakes the warm front (5–6), marking the first stage of the system's disintegration. The now-stationary front loses its punch (7), atmospheric pressure rises, the low-pressure core dissipates, and calm weather is restored.

Global Pressure Patterns and Alternating Climate Zones

By and large, the distribution of semipermanent areas of high and low pressure across the globe bears out Hadley's theory. The Earth's surface is divided latitudinally into fairly well defined climate zones, which in the Northern Hemisphere run south to north as follows:

The equatorial zone is a belt of relatively low pressure straddling the equator. Characterized by copious rainfall, it can shift as much as 1250 miles in either hemisphere or even creep across the equator. This movement influences climate over vast areas of the globe and is responsible for the punishing droughts that periodically parch the Sahel, the belt of land south of the Sahara.

The subtropical zone, including the areas of trade winds and the horse latitudes, is a belt of high pressure

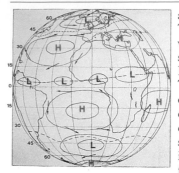

at about 25–35° latitude. This is where the world's great deserts, such as the Sahara and Kalahari, are located. The descending branch of the tropical Hadley cell in these regions creates a persistently sinking airflow that inhibits cloud formation. It is this pattern, not low humidity, which is primarily responsible for the lack of rain.

The temperate zone between roughly 35 and 50° latitude is a region of marked changeability. Highs and lows tend to follow in each other's wake along latitudinal paths largely dictated by jet-stream flow.

The boundaries of the low-pressure belt at about 50–60° latitude, also known as the polar front, shift with the seasons.

The polar caps of high pressure are permanent but also shrink and expand with the seasons.

The distribution of such high- and low-pressure areas is nearly identical in the Southern Hemisphere, only in reverse order.

Highs and Lows

We welcome highs because they are generally associated with calm, settled conditions and in summer do bring their share of fine, sunny days. In other seasons, however, they can mean weeks or even months of dreary, overcast skies. When the atmosphere is too stable and the air too still, wintertime fog can often be slow in lifting.

This occurs when the temperature, instead of decreasing with altitude as it normally would, increases, resulting in what is known as a temperature inversion. Depending on the season and temperature, an inversion layer can extend upward a few feet or as much as 6500 feet above the ground. Acting like a thermal lid that prevents warm air and smoke from rising, inversion layers not only prolong gray skies, but they allow impurities to build in the air by trapping everything close to the ground. The pollution index skyrockets.

Lows are no more a guarantee of bad weather than highs are of good. Under certain conditions, lows can bring unexpected changes for the better. If there is enough of an interval between disturbances, the rear sky behind a cold front can usher in extended periods of sunshine, the air cleansed of impurities by the recent precipitation. Fog and mist have been swept away. There is a marked improvement in visibility; sunlight feels warmer. The lingering memory of rain makes us appreciate the improved weather all the more.

Rising air in tropical regions encourages the formation of low-pressure areas along a belt straddling the equator (opposite). The return flow of sinking air farther north creates a zone of semipermanent high pressure in subtropical latitudes, where the Earth's great deserts lie.

The sun beats down on the Kalahari (left) more than four thousand hours every year, and the humidity hovers around ten percent. The exceedingly low moisture content of the air promotes nighttime cooling, resulting in such extreme differences between daytime and nighttime temperatures that rocks expand and contract substantially and eventually crack; they gradually break down to sand and dust.

Temperatures in the bleak, inhospitable polar regions routinely plummet to -50° C in winter and seldom rise above freezing in summer. Because of low humidity, snow falls not as large flakes but as an almost continuous shower of tiny ice crystals. The emperor penguin (center) is one of the few animal species capable of surviving such harsh conditions.

Clouds are made up of droplets of moisture so tiny that at least a million of them are needed to form a single raindrop. How do these droplets aggregate in the churning atmosphere and form rain, drizzle, snow, sleet, or hail?

CHAPTER III
THE WORLD OF CLOUDS AND RAIN

Thousands upon thousands of times all over the world, amateur weather watchers like this Englishman (right) patiently collect and measure daily rainfall. This chore is gradually being taken over by automatic weather stations.

Air is ceaselessly conveying water vapor to the Earth's surface, but its capacity to do so depends largely on temperature. The warmer the air, the more water vapor it can hold. But air can hold only so much vapor at a given temperature, and at a certain maximum point it is said to be saturated. Then the vapor condenses into microscopic droplets, releasing heat that allows it to keep rising. Furthermore, because air is constantly on the move, it can either cool down or warm up, depending on time and place. When it cools enough, it causes the water vapor it contains to condense out.

Latin in the Sky

Actually, water has trouble condensing into droplets in the air unless it has something to cling to. The tiny "condensation nuclei" it uses—usually specks of sea salt, dust, sand, or other airborne particles—are plentiful at the Earth's surface but can be in very short supply in the upper atmosphere. In fact, when air is perfectly clean, it can hold more water vapor than is theoretically possible. It is then said to be in a state of supersaturation.

Turbulent or serene, the sky is an ever-changing panorama of color because of clouds like the cumulus and stratocumulus scudding across Pierre de Valenciennes' splendid study of Roman skies (above). Most water droplets suspended in the atmosphere condense around particles of sea salt. The water cycle operates like an vast natural factory, transforming vast quantities of salt water in the oceans into water vapor aloft; it then falls as precipitation from clouds. The amount recycled represents only a small percentage of the world's stock of water, which has hardly changed since the beginning of time.

Clouds are aggregations of condensed water vapor suspended in the atmosphere. Clouds assume a limited number of shapes wherever they form over our planet, and each type allows observers to predict the weather a few hours ahead.

In 1803 Luke Howard, an English amateur weather watcher, laid the groundwork for the classification system still in use today. He assigned each cloud type a Latin name according to its general appearance: cirrus ("curl") for high, wispy, fibrous strands; cumulus ("mass") for flat-based heaps extending upward; and stratus ("spread out") for low, horizontal sheets. These three primary categories in various combinations became the basis for the ten main cloud families: cirrus, cirrocumulus, cirrostratus; altocumulus, altostratus, nimbostratus; and stratus, stratocumulus, cumulus, and cumulonimbus.

What Causes Precipitation?

Nearly all precipitation forms in clouds where the temperature is below freezing and there is a mixture of ice crystals and minute unfrozen water droplets.

It is natural to assume that water invariably turns to ice at subfreezing temperatures. In the upper atmosphere, however, something quite surprising takes place: Water can remain in a liquid state even below the freezing point. Such "supercooled" water

Cloud shapes are endlessly diverse and intriguingly beautiful. Some, like these lenticular altocumulus clouds (left), look like gigantic brushstrokes in the sky. In 1802 French naturalist Jean Lamarck first proposed a cloud classification system with five main divisions: hazy, massed, dappled, broomlike, and grouped. The Latin nomenclature that Luke Howard (below) devised for cloud types proved more popular. In 1887 English meteorologist Ralph Abercromby traveled around the world to make sure that clouds indeed looked the same everywhere. The 1891 International Meteorological Conference in Munich recommended that all weather services adopt an expanded version of Howard's classification.

High Clouds

Wispy or fibrous cirrus clouds (*Ci*) form at a relatively high 20,000 to 26,000 feet. Composed entirely of ice crystals, these benign, feathery filaments, which strong high winds sweep into hooklike "mare's tails," sometimes resemble jet contrails.

Wan, milky sunlight filters through a thin whitish veil of cirrostratus (*Cs*).

Tiny ice crystals form the closely spaced, pebbly elements of cirrocumulus (*Cc*). An encroaching "fish-scale" or "mackerel" sky is a sign that wet, stormy weather is approaching.

Mid-Level Clouds

Composed of water droplets 6500 to 16,000 feet high, the variably fibrous billows or rolls of altocumulus (*Ac*) give the sky a chaotic appearance and often precede thunderstorms.

Altostratus (*As*) is a fairly uniform, featureless sheet of

variably dense cloud. Thickening altostratus heralds approaching rain.

Thick, dark, ominous nimbostratus clouds block out the sun and reduce visibility. Rain or snow is imminent.

Low Clouds

When dreary stratus (*St*) blankets the sky with a uniform sheet of gray, the humid air produces occasional drizzle or very fine mist.

As its name indicates, stratocumulus (*Sc*) is an intermediate type with both stratus and cumulus features. The sun tries to peep through gaps between the closely packed clouds, which can produce light rain or snow.

Vertical Development Is a Sign of Instability

Although their flat bases lie just a few thousand feet above the ground, white, fleecy, "cotton-wool" cumulus (*Cu*) clouds develop vertically against the clear blue sky and reach altitudes of 16,500 to 20,000 feet, often forming "cauliflower" tops. Small or medium-sized cumulus are generally made up of water droplets, but when they build into the colder reaches of the atmosphere their tops consist of tiny ice crystals. Such towering clouds can produce showers.

The lowering undersurface of a cumulonimbus (*Cb*) can be ragged or frayed and develop blackish-gray pouchlike protuberances called mamma (left, center). The upper portion of these towering thunderstorm clouds spreads out, as if colliding with an invisible ceiling, to resemble an anvil.

FIG. 271. — Grêlons gros comme des oranges.

droplets are highly unstable and freeze into tiny ice crystals spontaneously when they come into contact with something solid. Then they must go through a series of stages in order to grow.

The first is transfer, a process that allows ice crystals to grow—as much as tenfold—at the expense of water droplets, which are continually evaporating. Once the growing crystals get relatively heavy, they start to fall. As they do, they continue to grow by coalescence. Supercooled water droplets collide with them and freeze, a process known as riming. As ice builds up on them, the crystals become heavier and fall even faster. They start to come together and form snowflakes.

However, the temperature of the air through which the snowflakes fall can vary, and it is what

happens to them on the way down that determines whether the precipitation will ultimately take the form of rain, snow, or hail.

Hailstones can be as big as oranges (above left). In 1959 one weighing over four pounds, the heaviest ever recorded, fell in Kazakhstan.

The Varied Faces of Falling Ice Crystals: Silent Snow and Dreaded Hail

When snowflakes pass through air with a temperature below the freezing point, or if they fall fast enough, they never melt and eventually reach the ground in their frozen form, as snow. Snowflakes are geometric aggregates of ice crystals. Because it traps a considerable amount of air, freshly fallen snow is roughly ten times less dense than water. The rule of thumb is that on average ten inches of snow is equivalent to one inch of rain.

Under different conditions, water droplets hook on to ice crystals too quickly for crystallization to occur, and the resulting frozen precipitation takes the form of particles of ice instead of snowflakes. Their ultimate

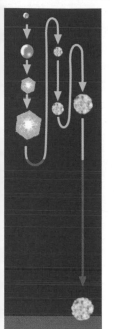

The water vapor in the atmosphere can change to either a liquid or solid depending on the temperature of the layers of air through which it passes (left). Surface temperature is of secondary importance in determining the precipitation's ultimate form. Snowflakes often arrange themselves hexagonally (below).

size determines their designation. Hard pellets no smaller than 0.2" in diameter are defined as "hail" or "hailstones." Smaller transparent or translucent spheroids or spicules are defined in the United States as "sleet," though this term has a different meaning elsewhere.

Meteorologists studied the composition, properties, and resistance of snow cover at a Siberian avalanche research station in January 1965 (left).

Indispensable Rain

More often than not, snowflakes quickly melt as they fall and turn into liquid drops of water, which then merge with others during their descent to form larger drops. When their diameter reaches about 0.25", they break up into droplets, and the process starts all over again. Thus, many raindrops can form from a single parent drop.

Fairly widely separated drops of water larger than 0.02" in diameter (or smaller ones with more space between them) are defined as rain. Liquid precipitation in the form of smaller, closely spaced droplets is officially designated as drizzle.

Dew and Frost Need No Clouds to Form

When surfaces near the ground get cool enough, the invisible water vapor in the air condenses on contact with them, forming tiny beads of visible water. Dew is most often seen early in the morning after a still, chilly night.

When the temperature of a surface drops to below freezing, the water vapor in the air will freeze instantaneously on it and form minute ice crystals called frost. Neither dew nor frost falls to the ground from clouds; they are deposited directly.

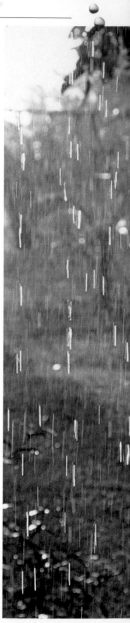

U sually associated with areas of high pressure, cooling during clear, still nights deposits dainty beads of dew on spiderwebs (below).

Warm, Cold, and Occluded Fronts

Within the atmospheric free-trade zone we call a depression or a low, cold polar air and warm tropical air meet head-on. In the Northern Hemisphere the warm air tries to force its way northward. As it strains against the cold air mass, a slight bulge develops, and the warm air, being lighter, starts to rise. The water vapor within the warm-air low-pressure area condenses into droplets, producing clouds all along the boundary between the warm and cold air. This wide band of cloud is called a warm front.

At the same time, but slightly to the west, the denser cold air starts to flow southward. As it does, it slides under the warm air ahead of it and pushes it up. This rapidly condenses water vapor and produces a narrow band of fast-rising clouds along the boundary between the contrasting air masses. This is a cold front.

If conditions are right, cold air may move faster toward the south than warm air does toward the north. When this occurs, a cold front will overtake a warm front and lift it so that it does not touch the ground, forming what is known as an occluded front or

While tropical regions receive as much as 10 to 13 feet of precipitation every year (center), other parts of the world are woefully shortchanged. Some deserts have experienced dry spells lasting up to ten years. In temperate regions, which are subject to significant variations in climate, floods may alternate with droughts severe enough to parch and crack a riverbed (opposite below, the Rhine, 1952).

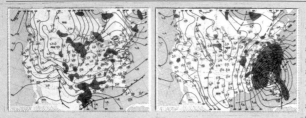

Maps track weather developments over three consecutive days as an enormous storm system forms and sweeps across the east coast, 12–14 March 1993. By the third day (opposite above), skies are clearing over much of Florida, while New England is experiencing heavy showers.

occlusion. These various processes can intensify and expand into vast cloud systems whose dimensions can be measured in hundreds of miles.

Anatomy of a Storm

Meteorologists refer to a large-scale system of warm, cold, and occluded fronts centered on an area of low atmospheric pressure as an extratropical cyclone, although the words "disturbance" or simply "storm" are often used. The theory of storm development is known as the Norwegian cyclone model because it

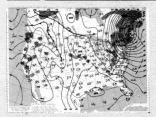

was first proposed by Norwegian physicists Vilhelm Bjerknes and Halvor Solberg in 1917, long before the advent of the satellites that so conclusively confirmed it. The theory is that eddies that develop along fronts grow into storms.

All middle-latitude cyclones were found to consist of three characteristic zones some call the fore, central, and rear skies. Each brings an immediate change in sky conditions, barometric pressure, wind direction, and temperature.

In the middle latitudes, three-quarters of all storms approach from the west. Because of the general circulation of winds in the upper atmosphere, storms from the north or south are unusual, those from the east even rarer. To get a clearer picture of how these

On many weather maps, the letter H (for high) indicates areas of high pressure; L (for low) marks areas of low pressure. Here, isobars are plotted at four-millibar intervals. Above: Combinations of blue triangles and red semicircles represent (top to bottom) cold, warm, occluded, and stationary fronts.

phenomena operate, let's imagine that a storm is bearing down on us from the ocean.

The Sky Clouds Over: A Front Is Approaching

The first sign of change is the appearance of high cirrus clouds: delicate, strandlike wisps or hooks

Fog and mist—tiny water droplets suspended in the air—reduce visibility. The supercooled droplets in "freezing fog" freeze on contact with objects, leaving a deposit of rime that makes for treacherous driving conditions.

that often escape notice because they do not obscure the sun.

Alert observers, however, will notice that the barometric pressure has begun to fall. The wind swings around to the south or southeast. ("When the wind backs and the weather glass falls, then be on your guard against rain and squalls," warns one traditional saying.) The shift in wind direction is accompanied by characteristic phenomena that vary from region to region: Fog dissipates, the smell from nearby factories intensifies ("When ditches and ponds offend the nose, look for rain and stormy blows"), and distant church bells can be heard more clearly ("Sound traveling far and wide, a stormy day will betide").

The temperature responds to various influences that can move it up or down depending on local conditions. In summer, it tends to rise as southerly winds start to blow, only to fall as the sky clouds over. In winter, the same cloud cover inhibits radiational cooling of the ground into the upper atmosphere and so causes the temperature at the surface to rise.

Little by little, the clouds knit together. A thin,

Cirrus clouds are often harbingers of rain. They begin as isolated wisps and build in the upper atmosphere, gradually marshaling themselves in ribbonlike formations up to six miles long. In time rippled cirrocumulus like these photographed over a tower in Nîmes, France (left), knit together and form a thin, whitish veil of cirrostratus cloud.

A canopy of umbrellas suddenly materializes to shield spectators at a tennis match in Wimbledon (below).

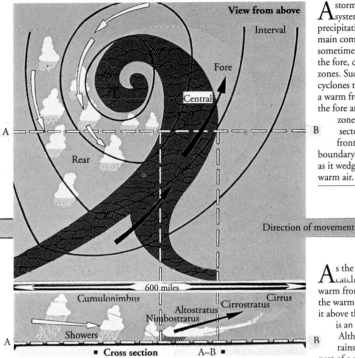

View from above

Interval

Fore

Central

A — — — — — — — — — B

Rear

Direction of movement

600 miles

Cumulonimbus

Cirrus

Altostratus · Cirrostratus
Nimbostratus

Showers

A — — — — — — — — — B

■ **Cross section**   A–B ■

A storm is an organized system of clouds and precipitation with three main components sometimes referred to as the fore, central, and rear zones. Such extratropical cyclones typically include a warm front between the fore and central zones, a warm sector, and a cold front marking the boundary of cold air as it wedges under the warm air.

As the cold front catches up with the warm front, it shrinks the warm sector and lifts it above the ground. This is an occluded front. Although it usually rains as the central part of a storm moves through, the first drops to fall from the clouds often evaporate well before they reach the ground. This precipitation, visible as shafts slanting down from cloud bases, is called virga. As the cloud cover continues to thicken and the air becomes increasingly humid, the raindrops complete their journey to the surface.

transparent veil of cirrostratus, mingled with varying amounts of cirrocumulus, spreads across the sky. Meanwhile, the barometer falls more quickly. The air becomes clearer, and visibility improves. In mountainous terrain, distant peaks appear to be nearer. ("The farther the sight, the closer the rain.")

Down Comes the Rain

The clouds lower and thicken, gradually forming a dense, grayish layer of altostratus. The first raindrops are felt. The cloud cover turns darker. The sky is blanketed with nimbostratus clouds, the serious rainmakers. The barometer continues to fall and then holds steady. The

wind turns blustery and
swings around to the west or
southwest. ("Southerly winds
with showers of rain,
will bring the wind from the
west again.")

The End of the Storm

The rain tapers off. The bases
of the nimbostratus clouds rise.
The first chinks of blue peep
through. The clouds break up

into increasingly
disorganized sheets
or banks. The
barometer does
an about-face
and rebounds
smartly. After
hesitating a
while, the
wind shifts
decisively north.
   A rapid, steady
rise in barometric
pressure means that conditions will remain more or
less settled. Lengthening bright intervals eventually
usher in a spell of sunny weather.
   Most of the time, however, improvement is slower
in coming. The atmosphere behind a cold front can
remain unstable, inducing cumulus formation and

-20° C

0° C

Surface of the Earth

TROPOPAUSE

ISOTHERM

showery weather. In extremely unstable conditions, such clouds can swell into spectacular cumulo-nimbus that have the potential to produce thunderstorms.

Deep Inside a Thunderhead

The giants of the sky, cumulonimbus are looming mountains of cloud capable of unleashing fierce thunderstorms and hail. Their bases usually lie about 3000 feet above the ground, and their tops can generally reach a height of up to 33,000 feet in midlatitudes. In tropical

As an ice pellet inside a cumulonimbus cloud (left) collides with more and more supercooled water droplets, it quickly takes on a coating of ice and begins to fall. But powerful updrafts pull it back up to the freezing part of the cloud, where it takes on another layer of ice and falls, only to be flung upward again. In cross section hailstones often reveal concentric growth rings that chronicle their life cycle. Fierce hailstorms frequently pelt the central plains of the United States (below).

De lapfu Pifcium, Ranarum, Murium, Vermium, & Lapidum.

regions, however, it is not unusual to see them tower 53,000 feet—more than nine miles—into the sky! At peak development, the upper reaches of a cumulonimbus spread out to the sides and form a characteristic anvil shape.

The raw material that fuels these thermodynamic powerhouses is warm, humid, unstable air. Cumulonimbus clouds suck in enormous quantities of moisture—hundreds of cubic miles of it—to feed their own growth. As water vapor is wrung out of the air,

Phenomena like this shower of fish in Scandinavia are known to have occurred from time to time. Powerful updrafts in developing cumulonimbus clouds can suck up small objects or animals and deposit them far away as it begins to rain.

Cloudlike swarms of locusts like the ones that ravaged southern Morocco in 1954 (left) migrate by riding favorable winds.

Tornadic activity can occur over an ocean or lake, producing waterspouts (right). The rapidly rotating vortex of air dipping down from a cumulonimbus is made visible by the water it picks up.

droplet condensation releases latent heat; the cloud builds ever higher. The insatiable cumulonimbus makes its awesome presence felt not only on the air it swallows up directly beneath it, but over an area that can extend many miles in every direction. The tremendous force with which these colossal vacuum cleaners suck in air can spawn small-scale, but unimaginably fierce tornadoes and waterspouts, spinning columns of air capable of obliterating everything in their path.

When such events occur, small objects (such as nuts) or even animals (such as frogs and fish) can be carried aloft and released miles away, resulting in the kind of astonishing shower that may have inspired the expression "raining cats and dogs."

In a Flash: The Sound and Light of Lightning

The electrical phenomena inside a cumulonimbus set it apart from all other clouds. At a certain altitude, water droplets within the cloud freeze. As a result, it consists entirely of ice crystals at the top and entirely of water droplets near the base. This contrast leads to a separation of electrical charge. Simply put, a large positive charge builds up in the upper regions of the cloud, and a negative charge builds up toward the bottom. When the potential difference between the charged areas becomes sufficiently large, there is a discharge of electrical energy, the gigantic spark we call lightning.

An electrical discharge between a charged cloud and the ground is called cloud-to-ground lightning. Storms can also produce lightning between two or more oppositely charged clouds (cloud-to-cloud lightning). A lightning flash within a cloud that has areas of opposite electrical charges is called intracloud

Lightning is an extra-ordinarily powerful phenomenon that can do tremendous damage. According to the World Meteorological Organization, lightning killed on average ninety-one people in the United States annually between 1967 and 1987. It is drawn to anything pointing up (church spires, antennas), prominent (isolated trees), or made of metal (including bracelets, above).

lightning. A lightning stroke can last as little as a thousandth of a second or over a full second in a series of jolts resulting from multiple discharges along the same path.

Lightning manifests itself both optically and acoustically. Thunder is caused by air surging outward around the electrical discharge. In a few thousandths of a second, lightning heats the air along its path tens of thousands of degrees, triggering tremendous expansion and then equally powerful contraction. The sudden changes in air volume produce a deafening roar we hear as a clap of thunder.

As a lightning bolt carries its electrical charge from a cloud to the ground, the air along its path becomes intensely hot, vaporizing liquid water instantly. The sudden heating creates explosive tension that exerts unimaginable force on confined spaces. That is why we hear a sharp, cracking sound whenever lightning strikes trees and similar objects.

Warm, unstable, moisture-laden air rising perpetually over the tropics fuels frequent thunderstorms (above, cloud-to-cloud lightning in Java) that are typically far more spectacular than those in midlatitudes (far left). Hardly a day goes by without thunder in the belt straddling the equator: Indonesia experiences no fewer than two to three hundred thunderstorm days annually. The violence, speed, and danger of lightning have long captivated the human imagination. The Romans associated it with the god Jupiter (left), and the ancient Greeks believed that Zeus vented his ire by hurling thunderbolts from Mt. Olympus.

Uncanny Light Shows in the Sky: Intriguing Rainbows, Halos, Glories, and Auroras

Few meteorological phenomena intrigued our ancient forebears as much as the beautiful and mysterious rainbow. Individual raindrops refract, reflect, and then refract the sun's rays once more,

dispersing its light into colors arranged in the same order as when a prism splits white light into bands of red, orange, yellow, green, blue, indigo, and violet. For a rainbow to be visible, certain circumstances must occur: the sun must be no higher than 52° above the horizon, rain must be falling from another part of the sky, and the observer must have his or her back to the sun.

Experience has long since borne out the familiar weather proverb, "Ring around the moon, rain is coming soon." Halos are circles of light around the moon or sun created by the bending and scattering of light rays as they pass through ice crystals in the high-level cirrostratus (or, less frequently, cirrus) clouds that herald warm-front rain.

The eeriest of all atmospheric optical phenomena may well be what is called the glory, which appears as colored rings you see around your head while looking at your shadow on cloud or fog below. To see a glory, you

A ghostly Swiss mountain looming in the sky? Shadows like the one observed in 1934 at Château-d'OEx (top) are rare but explicable optical phenomena.

B ombardment of the atmosphere by charged particles from the sun creates polar auroras (above)— and renders mariners' compasses useless. Auroral colors are similar to those produced by an electrical discharge in an inert gas.

usually have to be on a sunlit mountain (or in flight, when you will see your airplane's shadow on the clouds below). Most astonishing is the fact that two people standing side by side cannot see each other's glory; you're the show and the audience rolled into one. A glory's colors (always red to violet moving in from the outermost ring) are caused by the reflection and diffraction of sunlight as it passes through the water droplets in clouds.

The northern and southern lights, the aurora borealis and the aurora australis, usually appear as variously colored arcs, rays, or curtainlike ribbons or streamers at altitudes of over three thousand feet. Auroras are most often visible in polar regions because the Earth's magnetic field channels the flow of electrically charged particles from the sun toward these latitudes. In a process similar to what happens on a television screen, the electrons are accelerated and interact with air molecules in the upper atmosphere and "excite" them into producing a glow of colored light.

According to a 13th-century belief, anyone who walked beneath a rainbow's arc changed sex! Rainbows are no less captivating for having yielded up their secrets. Research has shown that the symbol of the Greek goddess Iris, messenger of the gods, is simply light that a curtain of raindrops refracts, reflects, and disperses into colors when we have our backs to the sun.

In ancient times, the wind was feared and respected as a reasoning superhuman force that could mete out reward and punishment. Storms and hurricanes were believed to be manifestations of divine displeasure. We have learned much about the workings of the wind since then, but when threatened with its devastation there is still little we can do except issue warnings.

CHAPTER IV
WHO KNOWS THE WIND?

Storms have long been a popular subject for painters. The sea is heaving, the wind is howling, and lowering storm clouds overhead portend imminent disaster (opposite). Right: A landlubber shudders as gusts whistle ominously through the trees.

The Greeks differentiated between wind directions and associated them with particular deities. They spoke of four principal winds, one for each of the cardinal points: Boreas, Apeliotes, Notos, and Zephyros were the gods of the north, east, south, and west winds, respectively. Aristotle added the four intermediate directions to this design. His eight-sided configuration was the basis for the Tower of the Winds in Athens (1st century BC), an

Bristling wind roses like this one (left) from an early printed atlas (Amsterdam, 1547) adorned compasses and nautical charts as well as bound collections of maps. As collateral directions were added to the four cardinal points, the number of spikes increased from four to eight and then to sixteen, twenty-four, and thirty-two. Many of these elaborate diagrams indicated for a specific location the relative frequency and strength of winds from different directions. Though undeniably intriguing as decorations, wind roses had limited scientific usefulness.

Opposite below: As these tourists visiting the Acropolis in Athens discovered, the wind can be most revealing when least expected.

octagonal structure crowned with a wind vane.

The Romans added sixteen collateral points to their wind rose, bringing the total number of potential wind directions to twenty-four.

The superhuman status accorded the winds in ancient times and the awe they long continued to inspire are reflected in popular names that have endured to this day.

Today we speak of the "masterly" mistral, the scorching sirocco, the fabled simoom, the dependable trade winds, or the "roaring forties," the name sailors apply to the stormy latitudes between 40° and 50° South.

Nothing but a Compensating Airflow

It took hundreds of years for people to grow accustomed to naming winds according to the direction from which they blew. Whatever the new designations lost in poetry and nobility they gained in ease of identification.

The real challenge, however, was figuring out what wind is, and wrong-headed ideas continued to obfuscate the issue as late as the 17th century: Why do leaves move? Because wind moves them? Isn't it just as logical to assume that moving leaves generate wind?

In 1640 Galileo proved that air had weight. Following his lead, a few years later Torricelli and Blaise Pascal demonstrated

B uilt in the 1st century BC by Andronicus of Cyrrhus, a Greek-born architect from Syria, the Tower of the Winds in Athens (left) housed a water clock and had a wind vane on its roof. The male figures in its sculpted frieze personify the characteristic weather associated with each of the eight winds (above, left to right): Boreas, Kaikias, Apeliotes, Euros, Notos, Lips, Zephyros, and Skiron.

that wind is nothing more or less than a mass of moving air. An example from everyday life may make this concept easier to grasp. When a tire bursts, the compressed air rushes outward. Exactly the same thing occurs in the atmosphere. Air seeks a path from areas of high pressure to areas of low pressure. This shifting of air is what creates wind.

Thus, wind has but one mission to fulfill: to restore equilibrium by redistributing pressure. The greater the difference in pressure between two areas, the stronger the compensating airflow will be. Advances in meteorology have shown that wind speed and direction are dictated simply by the position of low-pressure and high-pressure areas.

The Wind Cannot Defy the Spinning Earth Beneath It

Picture someone throwing an object from the North Pole. The projectile moves in a straight line, but while it moves the Earth beneath it is rotating. Consequently, to earthbound observers, it will seem to follow a curved path. Rotational forces have precisely the same effect on air masses. (See diagram on page 82.)

In the Northern Hemisphere, winds appear to be deflected to the right of their line of motion. A stationary observer on the ground sees them flowing in swirls instead of straight lines. Surface winds circulate inward and

counterclockwise around cores of low pressure, outward and clockwise around cores of high pressure. (In the Southern Hemisphere, where winds appear to be curving to their left, the circulation pattern around highs and lows is reversed.) These rotational forces, known as the Coriolis effect, strongly influence the way our atmosphere works. The fact that highs and lows govern the world's winds helps account for the close relationship between wind and air pressure as expressed in Buys Ballot's law, stating that surface winds blow in a direction very nearly parallel with lines of equal pressure (isobars). In other words, you can tell which way the wind is blowing at any given location simply by looking at the isobars on a weather map.

Easy-to-use hand anemometers give a direct reading of wind speed. The oldest wind-measuring instrument was devised in Italy in 1450.

Left: Scientists track a weather balloon to calculate wind speed and direction in the upper atmosphere. Opposite: Weathercocks fashioned from metal cutouts were a common sight in Europe from the Middle Ages until the 19th century. The design usually alluded to a trade or profession.

Local Wind Systems Are a Breeze

All local wind systems are created by the uneven solar heating of adjacent areas. During the day, as the slopes of hills or mountains absorb sunshine, the air directly in contact with them starts to rise as it becomes warmer, and therefore less dense and lighter, than valley air. Cooler air from the valley below rushes in to replace it, creating a breeze blowing up the slope. At night, the situation is reversed. With no sun to warm them, cooling mountain slopes cause the increasingly dense, heavy air directly above them to slide down into the valley, producing a breeze in the opposite direction.

Few people are as intimately familiar with the dynamics of moving air as glider pilots and hang gliders. Ascending currents of warm air, or thermals, form a few hours after sunrise, build to peak strength during the hottest part of the afternoon, and die out a few hours after sunset.

Solar heating affects land and bodies of water differently. Air over land warms and cools faster than it does over the sea. These temperature contrasts generate land (that is, offshore) breezes and sea (or

Winds in the Northern Hemisphere circulate counterclockwise around areas of low pressure. This principle, nowadays commonly referred to as the Coriolis effect, may seem implausible at first. Doesn't the wind blow in a straight line? Picture a cannon at the North Pole firing a shell aimed straight at London. It will take the projectile hours to reach its faraway target. Meanwhile, the Earth is rotating, and London will have shifted to the east by the time the shell starts to fall, so it will end up in the Atlantic. The same holds true for the wind, which seems to curve, because we on the Earth are moving relative to its path.

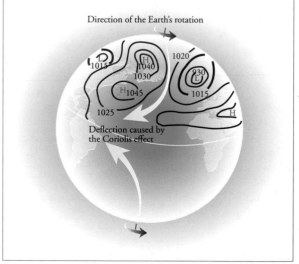

Direction of the Earth's rotation

1015 1040 1030 1020 930 1045 L 1015 1025 H

Deflection caused by the Coriolis effect

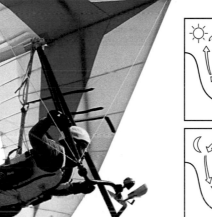

The sun heats mountainous or hilly terrain unevenly. As a rule, slopes catch sunshine, and valley bottoms remain in shadow longer. The resulting difference in temperature between crests and valleys causes a daytime breeze to sweep up the sunny side of a hill or mountain. Hang gliders soar by hitching a ride on rising thermal currents (left).

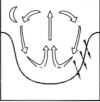

Glider pilots and hang gliders know that they cannot extend their flight time past a certain hour. As night falls and the air in contact with higher slopes becomes cooler and heavier, it begins to slide toward the valley floor, generating a breeze down the mountainside.

onshore) breezes. Coastal regions of oceans or large lakes have their own local wind systems, which can be a boon to windsurfers and sailors.

Such phenomena are especially noticeable in settled conditions associated with high pressure. In stormy weather, or simply in high wind, local breezes are masked completely by the overriding event.

When Wind Meets Mountain

When moving air encounters mountains or other such geographic barriers, it can do only one of two things.

First, it can flow around them and through the gaps between them. When funneled into a deep, narrow valley, airflow will speed up and cause wind to blow from a particular direction. Area residents long familiar with such behavior often give the wind a nickname that reflects its status as a local or regional phenomenon.

In most cases, however, air does not simply move around a barrier but ascends to hurdle it. Conditions may then be right for what is known as the foehn effect. Although its impact depends on local weather conditions and whether the topography involves gentle slopes, steep hillsides, or mountains, this variable phenomenon is often responsible for small-scale weather patterns known as microclimates.

The dynamics of foehn winds are such that the mere presence of a mountain can turn damp, cool air into warm, dry air. Amazing though it may sound, this transformation is in fact nothing more than an object lesson in textbook physics.

The Alchemy of Air: The Foehn Effect

As wind carries moisture-laden air higher up a mountainside, its temperature falls approximately a quarter of a Fahrenheit degree every 300 feet of elevation. Cooling causes the water vapor in the air to condense out, promoting cloud formation and occasionally depositing rain or snow on the windward side. Much of the air's water content is wrung out in the process.

Once it has spilled over the crest, the cooled, dehydrated air begins to tumble down the mountain, where it is warmed by compression, gaining heat at the rate of roughly one half a Fahrenheit degree every 300 feet it falls. The drier the air, the faster the rise in temperature. Thus, the air warms about twice as fast descending on the leeward side as it cools rising on the windward side.

Wind and topography can thus conspire to change the composition of the air from fairly cool and damp to

The different rates at which land and water build up heat create local breezes along coastlines. During the day, warm air rising over the land is replaced by cooler air flowing in from the sea, resulting in a cool onshore sea breeze.

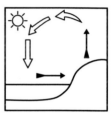

At night, warm air rising over the sea is replaced by cooler air flowing out from the land, which produces a mild offshore land breeze.

Airflow over geographic features becomes turbulent. The crests of orographic, or mountain-induced, waves are often marked by lenticular altocumulus clouds that look like flying saucers, stacks of dishes, or pancakes (left). Such clouds remain stationary relative to the ground even though a strong wind may be blowing through them. Thanks to the foehn effect (below), air can undergo a complete transformation simply by scaling a mountain. It starts out cold and humid on the windward side, dries out by the time it starts to spill down the leeward side, and then warms as it descends.

warm and dry. Consequently, opposite sides of the same mountain can experience radically different weather at the same time. One of the most dramatic examples of the foehn effect—named after the hot, dry winds that pour through Alpine valleys—is the chinook, a well-known wind that blows down the eastern slopes of the Rockies. In winter the rapidly warming air can cause rapid snowmelt and even trigger avalanches.

Comparative windward and leeward temperatures (° C) in otherwise settled conditions

ALTITUDE in meters

	Windward	Leeward
1500		
1400		
1200	6.5	6.5
1000	7.5	7.5
800	8.5	9.5
600	9.5	11.5
400	10.5	13.5
200	11.5	15.5
0	13	17.5
	15	19.5

This California farm has been generating its own electricity since 1960 by harnessing the power of airflow down the eastern slopes of the Sierras. Each wind turbine is hooked up to a generator.

Famous Winds

The United States is home to one of the most spectacular types of wind: the tornado. Tornadoes—whose most powerful winds can be twice as strong as a hurricane's

—do occur all over the world, but nowhere else with such frequency and violence.

Europe is home to many famous winds, one of the most famous of which is the mistral, which howls down over southeastern France. The combination of a low-pressure trough over the Mediterranean and south of the Alps—the Gulf of Genoa, to be precise—and a strong ridge of high pressure over Spain or the Atlantic funnels cold air from the north through the Rhône valley. This narrow corridor sharply accelerates the airflow, resulting in a massive stream of dry, cold air that comes roaring down the valley at speeds of fifty to sixty miles/hour or higher.

The autan is a famous southerly wind drawn from the Mediterranean into France's Garonne river valley. The oppressively hot sirocco blows dry, dust-laden air from the deserts of North Africa over the Mediterranean and as far north as the southern shores of Europe. The fierce easterly lombarde whistles through the Alps near the French-Italian border.

Blizzards sweeping down from the Arctic bring numbing cold and wind-driven snow that can reduce visibility to near zero. In March 1908 such frigid conditions in New York hampered efforts to fight a building fire on Broadway.

Another storied easterly wind, the hot simoom, rises off the Arabian desert and into Egypt and Libya. The humid easterly levanter blows somewhat more gently along the southern Alps and the length of the Mediterranean. In winter, the dry, cold north-to-northeasterly bora lashes the relatively warm waters of the Adriatic and Black seas with freezing air from the Caucasus, bringing snow and ice and whipping up waves.

The simoom (literally, "poisoner," below) is a hot, dry wind that can whip up terrific sandstorms as it sweeps over North African deserts from April to June and again from September to December.

HURRICANE HUGO
6 PM EDT
21 SEPTEMBER 1989
135 MPH   941 MB

WIND SPEED (MILES/HOUR)
Under 1
1–3
4–7
8–12
13–18
19–24
25–31
32–38
39–46
47–54
55–63
64–72
73 or higher

The Violence of Storms and the Beaufort Scale for Measuring Them

When the barometer is low and falling rapidly, the pressure gradient force—the size of the pressure difference and the distance between areas of high and low pressure—increases; isobars become more tightly packed together. The compensating airflow, seeking to balance out pressure differences, strengthens. Like a river that runs faster the steeper its grade, the flow of air from high- to low-pressure areas accelerates, reaching average speeds of sixty-five miles/hour or higher. It is officially designated a storm.

By international agreement, national weather services must issue storm warnings when wind speeds reach 10 to 11 on the Beaufort scale (see chart) because rough seas swept by extraordinarily high waves pose a threat to all ships in the affected areas.

Dreaded equinoctial storms are caused by an unhappy coincidence of two unrelated phenomena. The level

Hurricane Hugo, which battered the southeastern coast in September 1989. The eye is very easy to see in the center of the spiraling clouds.

English Rear Admiral Sir Francis Beaufort (1774–1857, top) devised a scale of numbers for sailors to measure wind force. The updated Beaufort scale (above) lists wind speeds, effects, and official World Meteorological

BEAUFORT NUMBER	EFFECTS OBSERVED AT SEA AND ON LAND	WMO DESIGNATION (1964)
0	Sea like mirror; smoke rises vertically	Calm
1	Ripples, no foam crests; vanes do not move	Light air
2	Small wavelets, crests not breaking; wind felt on face	Light breeze
3	Large wavelets, scattered whitecaps; light flags extended	Gentle breeze
4	Small waves, numerous whitecaps/small branches move	Moderate breeze
5	Moderate waves, many whitecaps, some spray/small trees sway	Fresh breeze
6	Larger waves, whitecaps, more spray/large branches in motion	Strong breeze
7	White foam blown in streaks/whole trees in motion	Near gale
8	Moderately high longer waves/twigs broken off trees	Gale
9	High waves, sea rolls/slight structural damage	Strong gale
10	Very high waves, visibility reduced/trees uprooted	Storm
11	Exceptionally high waves/rarely experienced on land	Violent storm
12	Air filled with foam, sea white with driving spray, visibility greatly reduced/extremely rare, widespread damage	Hurricane

of ocean tides varies with the changing alignment of the Earth, the sun, and the moon. Around the time of the equinoxes, the sun's and the moon's gravity can combine in such a way as to create an unusually strong tidal pull. The powerful winds and higher ocean swells associated with storms that tend to strike at these times of the year put coastal regions already vulnerable to astronomical high tides at even greater risk for widespread damage.

Organization (WMO) terms; an impassive tree frog (opposite), a popular weather predictor, looks on.

Wave height is crucial in assessing conditions at sea. The World Meteorological Organization sea state code used by sailors and meteorologists differs markedly from the Beaufort scale. It consists of ten numbers (0 to 9) and corresponding designations ranging from "glassy" and "slight" to "rough," "high," and "phenomenal." Wave systems can be observed and analyzed when the sea is not too stirred up. "Wind waves" are caused by the effect of local winds on the surface, and their general appearance is called "the sea." Waves that have gone hundreds, if not thousands, of miles beyond the winds that produced them are called "swells." The direction of swell propagation can be quite distinct from that of locally observed wind.

In Joseph Wright of Derby's 1790 impression of Shakespeare's *The Winter's Tale* (left), Antigonus looks on as the raging sea dashes a ship against the coastline.

Hurricane Warning!

A hurricane, typhoon, or—to use the meteorological term—tropical cyclone, is an intense, compact storm system, usually 125–300 miles in diameter, that forms around a core of extremely low pressure. The marked difference in atmospheric pressure generates unusually powerful winds more than 75 miles/hour, and often ranging from 90–150 miles/hour. Huge thunderstorm-producing cumulonimbus clouds spiral inward toward the hurricane's center, or eye, where the sea-level pressure is lowest. These swirling bands of cloud produce torrential rain.

To make matters worse, hurricane-force winds combined with low atmospheric pressure cause the sea to pile up near the eye, resulting in a storm surge of quite a few feet that can bring a sudden, flooding rise in water levels as the storm moves ashore. Such floods can have devastating effects.

The Birth and Death of a Hurricane

Hurricane formation depends largely on sea temperature. Vast quantities of tropical ocean water evaporate once its temperature reaches 26° C. The warm, moisture-laden air is carried aloft in a spiral of strong winds, forming huge clouds. As water vapor condenses into water drops, the associated release of latent heat warms the air even more, and the process repeats itself, continually adding "fuel" to the growing storm and making it self sustaining. Once a hurricane moves over land, the supply of warm, humid air is suddenly cut off, and it rapidly loses its punch; this is why coastal regions always bear the brunt of their devastating fury. Hurricanes have been known to weaken noticeably when they move over islands only to reintensify once they head back out to sea.

After World War II the U.S. Weather Service began to systematically monitor disturbances and storms. Intrepid pilots venture deep into hurricanes (above left), a tremendously risky undertaking. Tropical cyclones (above) are accompanied by torrential downpours and fierce winds of between 90 and 150 miles/hour.

Enormous belts of cloud spiral around a hurricane's small central area, or eye, where conditions are almost calm and the air pressure can sink to 990 or sometimes as low as 870 millibars. The eye shows up particularly well on mosaic satellite images, making hurricanes easy to spot. In 1992 Hurricane Andrew (below) wreaked havoc in parts of Florida and the West Indies.

The weather that humankind has for so long sought to comprehend, predict, and manage is a ceaseless interaction involving not just the sun, the Earth, and the atmosphere, but humankind itself. From the naive superstitions of days gone by to today's high-tech aspirations, we cling to the age-old dream of coaxing the elements to act in concert with our needs and desires.

CHAPTER V
MANAGING THE ELEMENTS

From the glass globe of the Campbell-Stokes sunshine recorder (right) to computer-generated wind maps (opposite), meteorologists have always had a variety of tools at their disposal. The science of meteorology has long appealed to low-profile artisan-researchers committed to learning more about the elements around us.

Early in the 20th century Norwegian meteorologist Vilhelm Bjerknes proposed a new approach: apply the laws of thermodynamics and fluid mechanics to the atmosphere in order to predict its state at some point in the future.

What sounded simple in theory proved inconceivably

Weather buoys (inset) monitor air and sea temperature, atmospheric pressure, relative humidity, and other measurable conditions.

complex once it was put into practice. Applying the laws of physics to the dynamics of our ever-changing atmosphere yields a set of equations that generally cannot be solved. The most mathematicians can do is make a series of successive approximations.

Here is the question in a nutshell: If we know enough about prevailing conditions now all over the world, can we predict weather developments for a few days ahead?

An Ever-Widening Observation Network

To learn as much as they can about prevailing conditions, meteorologists have developed an impressive worldwide observation network designed to monitor atmospheric phenomena as thoroughly and as accurately as possible. Ten thousand permanent land-based weather stations check conditions around the clock, as do another five

Vilhelm Bjerknes (left) was the first to think of the dynamics of the atmosphere in terms of the laws of physics and mechanics, but calculation technology at the time made his theories impracticable.

"I shall be more than happy if…I am able to predict the weather from day to day after many years of calculation. If only the calculation shall agree with the facts, the scientific victory will be won. Meteorology would then have become an exact science."
Vilhelm Bjerknes,
"Meteorology as an Exact Science,"
Monthly Weather Review,
1914

Meteorologists everywhere miss Point K, an observing station in the eastern Atlantic that used to operate from the *Carimaré* (left). This system proved too costly and was scrapped with the advent of weather satellites.

thousand aboard ships plying the world's oceans and seas. Commercial pilots continually radio back weather information encountered along their flight paths.

Supplementing these conventional techniques are unmanned devices (such as automated weather stations and weather buoys) that continually transmit local temperature, air pressure, humidity, and precipitation data. Nearly fifteen hundred radiosonde balloons are released every day to sample conditions in the upper atmosphere. In addition, many countries use weather radar to locate and determine the intensity of precipitation as it is falling.

Polar-orbiting and geostationary weather satellites have assumed pivotal importance in this network over the past twenty years. In addition to taking photographs and gathering indispensable data about cloud movement, upper-air wind speed and direction, and temperature patterns aloft, they serve as telecommunications links that transmit information from instruments to weather centers.

Sensors aboard polar-orbiting National Oceanic and Atmosphere Administration (NOAA) satellites (above) scan the atmosphere in different wavelengths simultaneously; the data are then processed as maps of upper-air temperature and humidity. Although sounding balloons make the same kinds of observations, satellites have greater information-gathering capability and monitor conditions in otherwise inaccessible areas, all at lower cost.

The French weather service's *Merlin IV*, a specially fitted weather aircraft, takes part in various measurement and research projects.

Lewis Fry Richardson: The Lone Genius of Numerical Forecasting

During World War I, English meteorologist Lewis Fry Richardson embarked upon a brand-new type of meteorological adventure. Using the observation network in place at the time, he tackled the mountain

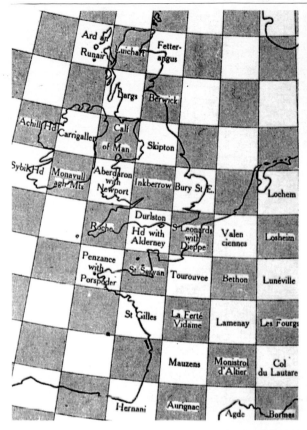

This Météosat satellite (above) is a geostationary satellite "anchored" 22,000 miles above the Gulf of Guinea. Its orbital speed matches the speed of the Earth's rotation.

Richardson devised a grid network to make the calculations he needed to make a numerical forecast. Pressure was measured at the center of each dark square and velocity in each white one. It was an ideal task for a computer, but in 1921 such machines did not exist.

of calculations needed to make a numerical forecast. Unfortunately, this Herculan task, which took several years to complete, ended in failure. It was later learned that his theories demanded highly refined calculation technology that simply had not yet been developed.

Richardson's error lay in figuring estimated values

Five geostationary satellites and two of NOAA's low-flying polar orbiters.

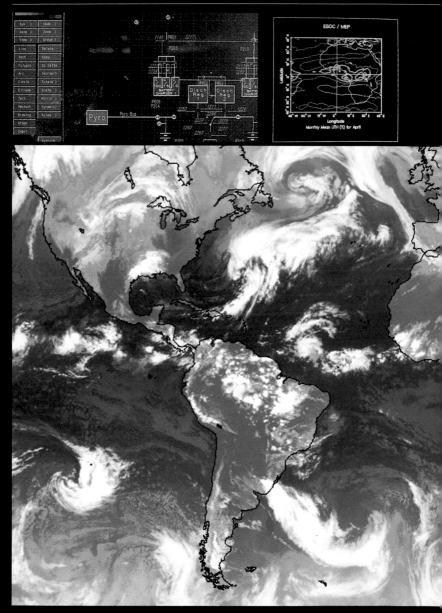

WV WINDS   20 JUL 93 2300

ACCEPTED
REJECTED

The Intertropical Convergence Zone —better known to sailors as the doldrums—shows up clearly as a band of white near the equator in this dramatic mosaic of photos that were taken by two Météosat satellites and computer enhanced to highlight areas of land, water, and cloud. Cloud photos are now among the least sophisticated of weather satellite products. In Europe information from Météosat satellites is transmitted to a 49-foot antenna in Germany that the European Space Agency's ground station keeps aimed at the satellite (below). It is then processed and evaluated on an impressive bank of monitors in the Darmstadt control room (left), including one for "steering" the satellites and others that plot upper-air humidity and wind vector data from Météosat's vapor and infrared channels (top, left to right).

based on six-hour intervals, and we now know that even an only marginally successful forecast requires that measurements be taken at intervals of thirty minutes at the most.

Richardson published his research in 1922. Calculating a meteorological prediction, he theorized, would require a colossal weather forecasting "factory" with 64,000 people working night and day. (See pages 146–7 for Richardson's own words on the subject.) In light of its disappointing track record, numerical weather forecasting was shelved for the time being.

A Tough Nut to Crack: Weather Prediction by the Numbers

In 1939 Swedish meteorologist Carl-Gustav Rossby went back to the equations and simplified and refined them so that they could be more easily used. After World War II advances in calculation technology provided some of the tools and the impetus for fresh attempts to implement Richardson's brilliant ideas. Weather prediction was the first "serious" problem computers were called upon to solve; it was also to prove one of the toughest.

In 1950 American mathematician John von Neumann of the Institute for Advanced Study in Princeton, New Jersey, published the results of his pioneering research in computerized numerical forecasting. Using a thirty-ton, 150-watt ENIAC digital computer—for all its bulk, complexity, and energy consumption, it was far less powerful than today's microcomputers—he generated simple model-driven forecasts that were comparable to those achieved by conventional synoptic techniques. The first hurdle facing the new technique had been cleared.

The complexity of early digital computers was mind-boggling (above left). The first was ENIAC, a behemoth consisting of forty-two units two feet wide, three feet deep, and almost ten feet high.

With advances in computer technology during the 1960s, numerical weather prediction finally hit its stride and subsequently became the basis for weather forecasting throughout the world.

But before you can run a numerical model—which consists of highly complex mathematical representations of various laws

B y the 1960s powerful computers had become a fixture at all major weather services; left, the director of the United Kingdom Meteorological Office, Bracknell, explains a Comet computer printout. Paradoxically, the explosive growth of computer technology has raised serious problems for meteorologists everywhere. It takes at least five years to develop increasingly complex weather models consisting of programs nearly 300,000 lines long. In the time it takes to complete this enormous task, the language may have become obsolete, or is about to. Are modelers therefore doomed to endlessly rewrite programs with which they have long since become intimately familiar?

of physics—you have to gather an enormous quantity of readings, measurements, and other data.

A Grid Mesh Around and Above Us

To make the calculation process as systematic as possible, the surface of the planet is divided into a mesh of equally spaced locations, or gridpoints. The atmosphere above is then divided into vertical levels, creating stacks of boxlike compartments. Once the three-dimensional grid has been laid out, the computer assigns values of atmospheric wind, pressure, temperature, and humidity to each gridpoint by statistically manipulating raw data from surface and upper-air networks. The accuracy of these initial conditions will largely determine how accurate a numerically calculated forecast will be. An enormously complicated series of mathematical operations is carried out, and the result is a simplified picture of the world's weather at a particular time. The gridpoints are currently set at sixty-two-mile intervals—still too widely separated for some small-scale weather phenomena, yet not so great a distance, considering that the grid mesh has to cover the entire planet. Equation solutions, generated as images and graphics (primarily maps) of anticipated wind, rain, and temperature patterns, are immediately passed on to most weather centers worldwide. Forecasters can then "fast-forward" the weather into the future by putting these simulations into motion on their computer screens.

Observation is One Thing, Prediction Another

Numerical forecasting gives its users an edge over amateur observers, skilled though they may be in monitoring and interpreting precursors of impending changes in the weather. Whereas synoptic meteorology infers the future movement of surface phenomena from wind and air pressure patterns alone, numerical models bring the atmosphere to life. Lows and highs form, intensify, and dissipate before the forecaster's eyes. The major services run daily computer simulations of anticipated weather patterns for a period up to ten days.

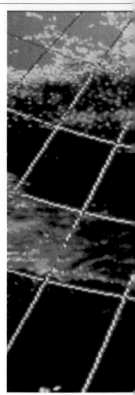

Caught in the meteorologist's net (above), the atmosphere is actually divided three-dimensionally into compartments stacked above the Earth (inset). Efforts are under way to more accurately represent weather phenomena by reducing the scale of the grids. The density of France's Arpège model (left) is variable: Note the concentration of gridpoints over western Europe.

Atmosphere

Earth

By providing a global picture of projected atmospheric conditions, numerical weather prediction models lend themselves to a wide range of practical applications. Shippers rely on forecasts of winds at the surface, and airplane pilots scrutinize predictions of winds aloft. Flood-warning services closely monitor predicted rain intensity. Gas and electric utilities evaluate temperature patterns. Farmers base their work schedules on anticipated weather conditions.

Observation First, Last, and Always

Computer models cannot generate viable climate predictions unless they factor in the oceans, a reservoir of incalculable energy that covers seventy percent of the Earth's surface. Meteorologists have deployed a virtual armada to monitor atmospheric conditions above the seas. Five thousand ocean-going ships (opposite above) send encoded observations on a regular basis in accordance with WMO standards. Unmanned drifting buoys (above left) fill out the picture by relaying information back to meteorological centers via high-flying satellites, observers in their own right that monitor cloud cover (above right) and other phenomena over areas where ships seldom venture. All weather data, regardless of source, are collected and transmitted worldwide through the WMO Global Telecommunications System by means of satellite antennas (left).

20°   10°W

SE Iceland

Faeroes

60°

Bailey   Fair Isle

Hebrides

Croma

For

Rockall   Malin

Shannon   Irish Sea

Fastnet   Lundy

50°

Sole   Plymouth   Port-
                          land

Finisterre   Biscay

40°

Trafalgar

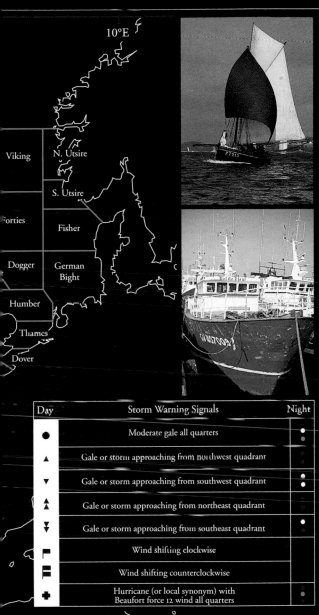

10°E

Viking

N. Utsire

S. Utsire

Forties

Fisher

Dogger

German Bight

Humber

Thames

Dover

They Also Serve Who Watch and Warn

All who work or play at sea rely on weather observations and forecasts for their property, if not their lives. In the United States, the National Hurricane Center, the National Meteorological Center, and the National Severe Storms Forecast Center gather information about and forecast storms of all sorts. While modern weather forecasting relies heavily on computer projections, the work of dedicated observers at signal stations (opposite) is still crucial. In western Europe all signal stations hoist storm warnings in accordance with international standards during the day; at night, they substitute a system of light signals for flags (left). To pinpoint locations, the region is divided into zones with which all sailors are familiar (center). Radio stations (antennas, opposite) broadcast regularly scheduled weather bulletins to listeners on the high seas. Pleasure craft and commercial trawlers alike (above left) closely monitor weather reports to chart optimum routes and learn of areas where the water temperature might attract schools of fish.

Day	Storm Warning Signals	Night
●	Moderate gale all quarters	::
▲	Gale or storm approaching from northwest quadrant	:
▼	Gale or storm approaching from southwest quadrant	:
▲▲	Gale or storm approaching from northeast quadrant	:
▼▼	Gale or storm approaching from southeast quadrant	:
┏	Wind shifting clockwise	
┏	Wind shifting counterclockwise	
✚	Hurricane (or local synonym) with Beaufort force 12 wind all quarters	::

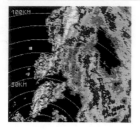

Correct Solutions Will Elude Even the Cleverest Mathematicians Unless the Starting Data Are Faultless

Impressive though our arsenal of high-tech data-gathering techniques may be, we still cannot ascertain prevailing conditions with pinpoint accuracy. Only by a pure fluke do observation stations ever lie exactly at intersections on the grid. There is no mathematical equation for calculating temperature, pressure, and humidity as variables of distance.

Knowing the air pressure in New York or St. Louis will not give you even a rough clue as to what barometers in Chicago read at that moment.

To complicate matters, observing stations are not evenly distributed over the globe: Coverage is good for the northern continents and the Northern Hemisphere but inadequate for the oceans and the Southern Hemisphere. The most computers can do is work by successive approximation. They assign "most probable" values to each intersection on the grid based on analysis of data from stations in the vicinity.

Since numerical forecasts use estimated

Weather radar can detect precipitation in progress within a 150-mile range and monitor its intensity, which is color enhanced on this screen (left) to show areas of heavier rainfall in red and lighter rainfall in blue.

values as their starting point, even scrupulously accurate mathematical calculations cannot help but yield an incomplete picture of future weather conditions. Small wonder, then, that the longer the forecast period, the more the results may diverge from reality. Meteorologists believe that, with the technology now at their command, the limit to detailed, day-by-day forecasts may be only six or seven days.

Many of the Atmosphere's Secrets Have Yet To Be Unlocked

In point of fact, numerical forecasting is "blind" and does not really explain anything. Causes and effects are so inextricably intertwined that we cannot describe in detail how atmospheric phenomena at the surface originate. Weather forecasters are little more than enlightened bystanders. They look on as lows and highs deepen or dissipate, and draw on their experience to calculate the odds that any given scenario will unfold as predicted.

For the last twenty years or so, the development of increasingly powerful computers has led to a steady improvement in forecasting skill—a gain, many meteorologists estimated, of roughly one day every five years. But could factoring in an ever-growing number of phenomena on an ever-shrinking scale go on indefinitely? Might numerical techniques exhaust their potential one day, necessitating fresh approaches or new technologies for long-range forecasting? These and similar questions came

What looks for all the world like a satellite photo of western Europe (below) is in fact a composite image created by superimposing an upper-air infrared radiation scan over a map. If the computer simulation is accurate, the areas in white should match actual cloud cover.

Investigating the atmosphere calls for resourcefulness. Meteorologists have always availed themselves of the most advanced technology at their command, from dial instruments (like the ones this technician is using in 1930 to monitor upper-air temperature fluctuation, left) to satellites and computer-generated images used today.

to the fore as meteorologists began to ponder a controversial issue: Is the atmosphere "deterministic," that is, determined by earlier events or natural laws? Stated differently: Can we ever expect to know what the weather will be whole months ahead of time?

The Flap of a Butterfly's Wings

It was long taken for granted that if meteorologists started with only slightly inaccurate data, their forecasts would prove only slightly inaccurate. But this "axiomatic truth" came under fire.

In 1963 Edward N. Lorenz, an American theoretical meteorologist at MIT, showed that the dynamics of the atmosphere are in fact heavily dependent on initial conditions and, therefore, that these dynamics vary wildly depending on the most minor differences in weather. He noticed that when he entered a set of starting numbers to six and then to only three decimal

places, his computer predicted markedly divergent weather patterns, not at all a virtual duplication. In other words, even a tiny atmospheric event could cascade through the system and have drastic consequences. To paraphrase the thought-provoking title of Lorenz's now-famous paper, a butterfly flapping its wings in the Amazonian rain forest could conceivably set off a storm somewhere else in the world a few months later.

Lorenz's groundbreaking research in what came to be known as chaos theory, or the Butterfly Effect, led many meteorologists to conclude that no matter what method they used, detailed, day-by-day forecasts beyond two weeks would be impossible not because of the complexity of the system, but because of its very structure. The inherent unpredictability of weather

After performing countless calculations, computer models generate short-term projections for all weather parameters. This map of moisture in the upper atmosphere (left) is color-coded to indicate relative humidity. Wherever it reaches 100 percent (red), clouds are considered a certainty and rain a strong likelihood. Information from other sources will show whether or not the anticipated pattern was correct.

threw up what many mathematicians, physicists, and meteorologists felt might be an insurmountable obstacle. After all, even a more-straightforward deterministic model requires both expertise in the atmosphere's laws and detailed, accurate knowledge of conditions at the start of a given forecast period.

The Vagaries of the Sun

The real stumbling block to reliable long-term weather prediction may prove to be the passage of time itself. The atmosphere is decisively influenced by patterns that take not just scores or thousands but in some cases millions of years to unfold.

Predicting changes in the atmosphere is as tricky as describing the dynamics of cigarette smoke. We can calculate the behavior of the first wisps, but things quickly become too complicated to describe. The merest breath of wind, and the smoke moves in a totally unexpected pattern. Lorenz showed that even assuming an exhaustive knowledge of initial conditions—an absolute necessity for reliably simulating future trends —the atmosphere behaves randomly beyond a certain point. He announced his findings in a 1979 paper with an unforgettable title. "Predictability: Does the Flap of a Butterfly's Wings in Brazil Set Off a Tornado in Texas?"

The 1960 launch by the U.S. of *Tiros 1*, the first weather satellite, marked the dawn of a new era. Photographs of cloud cover proved a valuable forecasting tool. Left: An American meteorologist preparing weather maps with the help of satellite photos. The range of tasks satellites perform has widened considerably. Their radiation scans are used to plot thermal profiles of the atmosphere.

Some involve the sun, others the Earth itself. In any event, timescales of that magnitude dwarf even the most ambitious of forecast periods. To evaluate the impact of extremely long-term cyclical patterns on a short-term, near-future framework, meteorologists have had to draw on the theory and practice of astronomy, geology, volcanology, physics, climatology, and other sciences. Factoring in the Butterfly Effect—numerical forecasting's inherent inability to deal with weather's nonlinearity, or chaos—leaves meteorologists with no alternative but to rethink their tools and methodology, if not the very way

The paintings of Peter Breughel the Elder (above, *Hunters in the Snow*) suggest what life was like during the period between the 15th and 19th centuries known as the Little Ice Age. Astronomers suspect that recurrent spells of harsh climate are caused by a fluctuation in the solar cycle every 314 years.

they reason, if ever they are to understand and predict weather and climate.

Ancient Chinese astronomers kept records of spots that appeared on the surface of the sun from time to time. Galileo confirmed their observations with his telescope in the 17th century. These patches span thousands of miles and are on average 2000° C cooler than the surrounding surface. Sunspots have a negligible effect on solar radiation, reducing it a scant 1 watt per square meter. In the 19th century, a German amateur astronomer, Heinrich Schwabe, discovered that periods of sunspot activity followed a cycle that averaged eleven years. Yet, weather records showed no such eleven-year patterns.

Since then, astronomers have learned that the cycle of solar activity is subject to irregularities. Every three hundred years or so, the sun balloons and its diameter swells by some 1200 miles. It spins less rapidly on its axis, and its brightness diminishes. Consequently, the Earth receives slightly less radiation, and the amount of solar energy reaching the outer layer of the Earth's atmosphere drops by about one percent. These temporary periods of solar weakness last about seventy years. Year after year, the cumulative shortfalls can add up to an appreciable amount of energy.

Not As Round As We Think

The Earth's diameter is about twenty-five miles greater along the equator than it is around the poles, so the

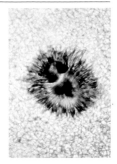

Sunspots are associated with periods of increased solar activity. As yet, there is no conclusive evidence that they influence the Earth's climate.

"Father Scheiner, a Jesuit priest from Ingolstadt, was the first to investigate sunspots. After making repeated observations, he consulted with his superior. 'Calm down, my son,' he told him. 'What you take for sunspots are defects in your lenses or your eyes.'"
Camille Flammarion
Popular Astronomy, 1880

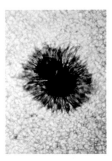

planet has a somewhat flattened shape and a slight equatorial bulge. Because of the varying gravitational attraction of the moon and the sun on the Earth's bulge, our planet does not remain perfectly steady as it rotates on its axis: it "wobbles," rather like a spinning top. Factoring in the gravitational influences of other

In 1930 Dr. Charles Abbot (below center) of the Smithsonian Institution discovered that the amount of radiant energy produced

planets, it takes about 22,000 years for the Earth's axis to complete a single revolution. One of the most important effects of this motion, called the precession of the equinoxes, is that the position of the equinoxes and solstices varies on the ellipse of the Earth's orbit. Consequently, the distance between the Earth and the sun varies for any given season, which in turn affects not

by the sun varies daily; the Earth's temperature responds to these changes. He invented the silver-disk pyrheliometer and the pyranometer, still used to measure global radiation.

only the thermal range between seasons, but probably also the polar ice caps.

Moreover, this wobble is never exactly the same from one revolution to the next because the tilt of the Earth's axis relative to the plane of its orbit undergoes a slow oscillation. The gravitational pull of surrounding planets causes it to "nod" between 65.5 and 68.2° over a period of 41,000 years. And as we have seen, the tilt of the Earth's axis is responsible for the uneven distribution of the sun's heat across the Earth's surface.

In the 1930s Milutin Milankovich, a Yugoslavian mathematician and physicist, computed from all of these factors a solar radiation curve and

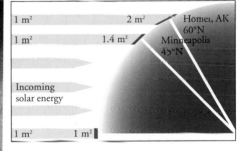

1 m² 2 m² Homer, AK 60°N
1 m² 1.4 m² Minneapolis 45°N

Incoming solar energy

1 m² 1 m²

calculated its effect on the amount of solar radiation available in different regions of the world in different seasons. Recent evidence about past ice ages

Incoming radiant energy from the sun strikes different latitudes at different angles, and the associated uneven heating of the Earth's surface causes variations in temperature. One square meter of surface area at the equator receives the same amount of energy as two square meters in Homer, Alaska (diagram left).

Because the Earth's yearly orbit around the sun is elliptical, its distance to our solar system's central star varies. At the present time, the Earth is farthest from the sun during the northern summer; but the situation was reversed 13,000 years ago, when it was farthest away in winter. The Earth's axis slowly gyrates, describing a cone in space with a rotation period of 26,000 years (diagram below). This "wobble" alters the amount of radiation reaching the Earth from the sun and causes significant climate changes, including, in all probability, the great ice ages. In the diagram the arrow around the equator indicates the direction of the Earth's rotation, and the yellow bars represent incoming solar energy.

1 2 3 4 5

(cores drilled in seabed sediments) has confirmed many aspects of Milankovich's astronomical theory of climate change.

The Fury from Within the Earth

So stupendous is the force of an erupting volcano that the jolt from the cataclysmic eruptions of Indonesia's Mt. Tambora (1815) and Krakatau, near Java (1883), was felt in distant lands. During these titanic events, plumes of hot water, vapor, ash, and rock can billow up as much as 65,000 feet into the air and hurl an estimated 10 to 100 million tons of dust into the atmosphere. Because it reduces the amount of sunlight reaching the surface, this massive injection of dust affects world climate. The surface temperature of the Earth is thought to have decreased on average about 0.5° C during Tambora's eruption—the force of which blew about four thousand vertical feet of the mountain's top away. Unusually cool, rainy weather persisted over many parts of the world in 1816, which came to

The 1991 eruption of the Philippines' Mt. Pinatubo hurled a plume of ash into the air (left). Stratospheric winds spread a belt of sulfur dioxide particles around the world (NASA photo, below), and the material affected both the composition and intensity of solar radiation.

be known as "the year without a summer." More recently, the eruption of Mt. Pinatubo in the Philippines in June 1991 threw a colossal plume of dust into the stratosphere, where winds spread it around the

EQ

Earth. Its short-term effect was to distort all satellite readings and garble images.

It should be emphasized, however, that as a rule the impact of such light- or heat-altering events is not long-lived. The climate cools for two or three years, after which equilibrium is restored. Volcanic eruptions may not be critical weather changers, but they do demonstrate that our planet's climate is neither

Krakatau in Indonesia released tens of millions of tons of dust during its eruption in 1883 (opposite). The resulting changes in upper-air composition led to several years of global cooling and produced atmospheric optical phenomena.

unresponsive nor unchanging. It can be disturbed to varying degrees by natural phenomena that are completely beyond our control.

Trying to Control the Weather: Making Clouds and Fighting Frost

Our forebears resorted to superstitions, processions, and prayers to coax the heavens into complying with their wishes. With the advent of science, the means may have changed but the objective has remained the same.

Greater understanding of certain atmospheric processes has inspired attempts to simulate nature in a number of specific ways. Cloud formation has been induced by burners, brushfires, and other techniques designed to heat the air in the lower layers of the atmosphere. Since some "cold" clouds were found to consist entirely of supercooled water droplets (and therefore lacked the amount of ice crystals necessary to trigger the formation

Benjamin Franklin (above) invented the lightning rod, a rare example of consistently effective weather modification.

The Météotron, a cloud-seeding process, was tested in the 1960s (top and bottom). It confirmed theories about cloud formation but also demonstrated our inability to muster the energy needed to create even a few respectable clouds.

It is tempting to resort to "magic bullets" (mobile hail cannon, below) when so many weather and climate phenomena are still so poorly understood, if at all. Overleaf: Workers in early-20th-century Italian vineyards waged an unrelenting war against hail, but their rockets proved no match for cumulonimbus clouds.

of precipitation), similar crystals were introduced artificially into the clouds with mildly encouraging results: Seeding clouds has met with only limited success in producing rain.

Some attempts at weather modification have proven more successful than others. Notwithstanding the wide range of protective measures available to them, farmers and fruitgrowers have yet to claim victory in their never-ending battle against frost. They have tried planting in low-lying areas, wrapping plants with cloth to prevent heat loss, creating artificial fog, using oil-burning stoves or smudge pots to warm the air, and circulating the air with large fans to prevent freezing. The problem is not lack of ideas but difficulty in implementing them.

In the final analysis, the only weather modification device that has shown itself to be completely and consistently effective is Benjamin Franklin's lightning rod.

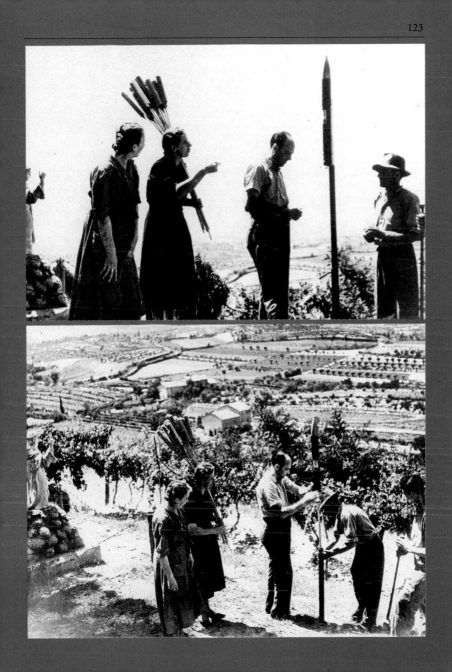

The Greenhouse Effect

For centuries gardeners have been creating greenhouse microclimates to stimulate plant growth. Plastic sheeting or panes of glass let sunlight in; the soil and plants absorb solar energy. They in turn emit infrared radiation, but infrared does not have the same wavelength as solar radiation and cannot penetrate glass or plastic barriers, so the heat has nowhere to go. This heat trapped inside the greenhouse builds and so keeps the temperature inside higher than it is outside. The artificially induced warmth and humidity encourage plant growth.

Ozone, a gas formed in the stratosphere, is extremely diffuse: If compressed at normal air pressure, the ozone layer would only be .01" thick. But it is essential to our existence because it shields us from the sun's harmful ultraviolet

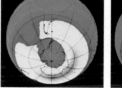

All bodies emit radiation. The intensity of the infrared radiation they give off depends solely on their temperature. This relationship is particularly remarkable in that it enables calculations to be made in the other direction: By measuring the amount of outgoing infrared radiation, we can determine the temperature of its source.

radiation. Ozone concentration over the poles appears to be steadily decreasing with each passing year.

The greenhouse effect began the day the atmosphere enveloped the Earth. It is essential to life but could lead to a warming or cooling of the Earth's climate if not kept within certain limits.

Incoming solar energy

340

Reflected back into space

100

70

Absorbed by clouds

240 Radiation emitted into the atmosphere

Atmosphere

Clouds

400 Infrared radiation emitted by the Earth's surface

330 Trapped radiation

100 Heat transfer (rising air masses)

170

In average number of watts/square meter of energy absorbed or lost

Our Atmosphere, Our Shield

The situation in a gardener's greenhouse is analogous to the interaction between the sun, the Earth, and the atmosphere. Incoming solar radiation passes directly through the layers of our atmosphere. The Earth's surface absorbs some of this radiant energy. But the Earth radiates away infrared energy, too (at a rate of about

Color-enhanced *Nimbus 7* satellite images show the growing hole in the ozone layer over the South Pole in October of 1979, 1981, 1983, 1985, 1987, and 1989 (the purple and black areas show the greatest

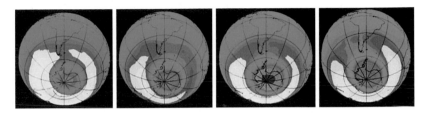

22 watts/square foot, according to satellite measurements). If this thermal radiation were lost to space, surface temperatures would climb no higher than -18° C. Fortunately, nine-tenths of the outgoing energy is absorbed by the water vapor, clouds, and carbon dioxide in our atmosphere.

Thanks to the greenhouse effect, the Earth's average surface temperature is a relatively mild 15° C. By

drop in ozone levels). Since depletion seems to speed up in September and October and replenishment occurs the rest of the year, the destruction of the ozone layer is thought to be seasonal. What worries scientists is that every year the hole is slightly bigger than it was at the same time the previous year.

Greenhouses duplicate the dynamics of the greenhouse effect. The plastic sheeting works much as our atmosphere does.

the same token, if the Earth did not shed some of the energy it absorbs, the heat would quickly build to unbearable levels. On the planet Venus, where the atmosphere is almost pure carbon dioxide, the surface temperature hovers around an unlivable 450° C! Therefore, our very existence hinges on a limited greenhouse effect, which in turn is largely contingent on the right "dose" of carbon dioxide in the atmosphere. If carbon dioxide levels were to rise significantly and intensify the greenhouse effect, it might well mean the end of life as we know it.

For the First Time in History, It Lies Within Our Power to Substantially Change the Course of the Global Climate

Industrial activity and automobile emissions, compounded by the effects of deforestation, introduce 20 billion tons of carbon dioxide into the air every year. According to the World Meteorological Organization, the impact of nitrous oxide, methane, ozone, chlorofluorocarbons (CFCs), and other gases

A smog research center was established in the Ruhr, Germany, in 1965 (above left): It was a sign of the times. The pollution problem became so critical that most major cities now continuously monitor air quality. A combination of unusually adverse meteorological conditions and smog claimed an estimated four thousand lives in London in 1952 (above center). Today's weather forecasts often contain information about air quality.

could be just as far-reaching. A buildup of these gases in our atmosphere would affect solar radiation and influence global weather patterns.

If emissions continue at current rates, greenhouse gas levels are expected to double by about the year 2050, a plausible enough scenario in light of statistics from the past few decades. Computer models run in the United States, England, and France generally agree that the Earth would suffer a "heat stroke." According to the most reliable estimates, the Earth's temperature would rise an average of 1.5° to 4.5° C. But this is nothing more than a general assessment. The projected distribution of additional warmth varies considerably depending on the particular climate model we use. Even if we assume that global warming is inevitable, it is extremely difficult to foresee, much less measure, its potential consequences. Does that make the need for precautions any less urgent?

Uncontrolled burning of fossil fuels and a ring of high mountains surrounding this high altitude city conspire to make Mexico City one of the most polluted urban areas on Earth.

Overleaf: An airport wind sock indicates wind direction.

DOCUMENTS

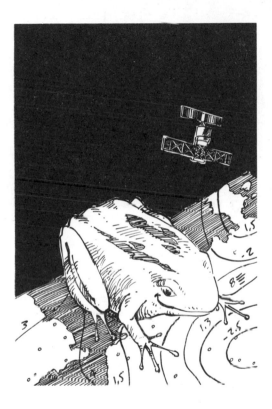

The Dawn of Meteorology in Ancient Greece

As far back as the 6th century BC, Thales of Miletus stated that the moon shines by the light of the sun. Another Ionian philosopher, Anaximander, described wind as a "flow of air" and argued that friction between clouds produced thunder. In the next century Anaxagoras held that lightning was triggered when part of the ether came crashing down. Ancient meteorology was breaking away from mythology.

Through the historian Herodotus the Greeks learned of the variability of climate, the inexplicable floods of the Nile, and the icy wind that raked the steppes north of the Black Sea. The 5th–4th-century BC physician Hippocrates, author of Airs, Waters, and Places, *strongly recommended studying the atmosphere and its vicissitudes because he believed that all living things were environment-sensitive. Legend has it that the 5th-century philosopher Empedocles earned the nickname "master of the winds" by sewing donkey hides together and stretching them across a mountain pass to shield the inhabitants of Agrigentum from the reputedly disease-bearing Etesian winds. Around the same time, Democritus applied his atomic theory of the nature of the physical world to atmospheric dynamics and*

A 17th-century German depiction of the wind.

suggested that storms move across the Earth's surface.

Science left its imprint on the Greek world by way of meteorology, which acquired such prominence it even inspired Athenian comic poets.

Aristophanes, Zeus, and *The Clouds*

In Aristophanes' comedy The Clouds *(423 BC), we meet a character named Socrates, but this sophist (sophists were a favorite target of the poet) has little in common with the historical Socrates.*

SOCRATES: Come forth, come forth,
  ye worshipful Clouds, present
  yourselves to sight,
Whether ye sit snow-crowned on
  Olympus' sacred height,
Or in your father Ocean's glade make
holy Nymphs to dance,
Or from the outpourings of River Nile
  dip waters that entrance,
Or whether you Lake Maeotis keep or
  Mimas' snowy tor:
Receive our offerings, heed our prayer,
  'tis you we all adore....
CHORUS OF CLOUDS: Greetings, old
  man, who seek the science of subtle
  speech!
And you, too, priest of cobweb folly;
  say what you wish.
No sophist high-flown would we rather
  oblige....
STREPSIADES: O Earth! what an
  awesome and portentous sound!
SOCRATES: They alone are deities, all
  the others nonsense.
STREPSIADES: But Zeus on Olympus,
  by Earth, is he no god?
SOCRATES: What Zeus? Don't be silly;
  there is no Zeus.
STREPSIADES: No? Then who rains?

First tell me that.

SOCRATES: These clouds, of course, and
I'll prove it by evidence plain.
Come, did you ever see rain without
clouds? But Zeus should bring rain
From a clear sky, when clouds are
vacationing.

Aristophanes
The Clouds
in *The Complete Plays of Aristophanes*
trans. Moses Hadas, 1962

"Matters of Which I Do Not Pretend to Know Either Much or Little"

*In the literary sense, an apology implies
no sense that wrong has been done; it is
simply an explanation or clarification
of the author's point of view. In Plato's
3rd-century BC Apology, he presents
Socrates' defense of himself at his trial
before the Athenian government.*

Aristotle, 16th-century engraving.

I will sum up [the slanderers'] words in
an affidavit: "Socrates is an evil-doer,
and a curious person, who searches
into things under the earth and in
heaven, and he makes the worse appear
the better cause; and he teaches the
aforesaid doctrines to others." Such
is the nature of the accusation: it is
just what you have yourselves seen in
the comedy of Aristophanes, who has
introduced a man whom he calls
Socrates, going about and saying that
he walks in air, and talking a deal
of nonsense concerning matters of
which I do not pretend to know either
much or little—not that I mean to
speak disparagingly of anyone who
is a student of natural philosophy. I
should be very sorry if Meletus could
bring so grave a charge against me.
But the simple truth is, O Athenians,
that I have nothing to do with
physical speculations. Very many of
those here present are witnesses to the
truth of this, and to them I appeal.
Speak then, you who have heard me,
and tell your neighbors whether any of
you have ever known me hold forth
in few words or in many upon such
matters.... You hear their answer. And
from what they say of this part of the
charge you will be able to judge of the
truth of the rest.

Plato
Apology
trans. B. Jowett
1969

Aristotle and His *Meteorologica*

*Aristotle's writings weave together a
number of conceptual threads, including
Empedocles' doctrine of the four elements
(air, earth, fire, and water), the ideas
espoused by his teacher Plato, and the
materialistic atomism of the Milesian*

A 17th-century engraving of Thales of Miletus.

school. His Meteorologica, *the first comprehensive treatise on meteorology, dates from about 334 BC.*

Let us next deal with the region which lies second beneath the celestial and first above the earth. This region is the joint province of water and air, and of the various phenomena which accompany the formation of water above the earth. And we must deal with their principles and causes also.

The efficient, controlling and first cause is the circle of the sun's revolution. For it is evident that as it approaches or recedes the sun produces dissolution and composition and is thus the cause of generation and destruction. The earth is at rest, and the moisture about it is evaporated by the sun's rays and the other heat from above and rises upwards: but when the heat which caused it to rise leaves it, some being dispersed into the upper region, some being quenched by rising so high into the air above the earth, the vapor cools and condenses again as a result of the loss of heat and the height and turns from air to water: and having become water falls again onto the earth. The exhalation from water is vapor; the formation of water from air produces cloud. Mist is the residue of the condensation of air into water, and is therefore a sign of fine weather rather than of rain; for mist is as it were unproductive cloud.

This cycle of changes reflects the sun's annual movement: for the moisture rises and falls as the sun moves in the ecliptic. One should think of it as a river with a circular course, which rises and falls and is composed of a mixture of water and air. For when the sun is near the stream of vapor rises, when it recedes it falls again. And in this order the cycle continues indefinitely. And if there is any hidden meaning in the "river of Ocean" of the ancients, they may well have meant this river which flows in a circle round the earth.

Moisture then is always made to rise by heat and to fall again to the earth by cold; and there are appropriate names for these processes and for some of their sub-species—for instance when water falls in small drops it is called drizzle, when in larger drops, rain.

Aristotle
Meteorologica
Book I, Chapter 9
trans. H. D. P. Lee
1952

The Wisdom of Weather Lore

Often expressed as rhyming couplets, weather sayings and proverbs evolved into a kind of folk science. Even when farfetched and unfounded, these gems of practical wisdom are an entertaining blend of tradition, popular belief, and superstition.

Popular depictions of weather, 17th century.

Ant: Ants that move their eggs and climb,
Rain is coming anytime.

Bear: A bad winter is betide
If hair grows thick on a bear's hide.

Bee: When bees stay at home, rain will soon come;
If they fly away, fine will be the day.

Cat: If the cat washes her face over her ear,
'Tis a sign the weather will be fine and clear.

Cirrus: Trace the sky the painter's brush,
The winds around you soon will rush.

Dew: When the dew is on the grass,
Rain will never come to pass.

Donkey: When the donkey blows his horn,
'Tis time to house your hay and corn.

Flea: When fleas do very many grow,
Then 'twill surely rain or snow.

Fly: A fly on your nose, you slap and it goes;
If it comes back again, it will bring a good rain.

Gnat: The gnats bite and I scratch in vain,
Because they know it is going to rain.

Goose: The goose and the gander begin to meander;
The matter is plain: they are dancing for rain.

Grass: When grass is dry at morning light,
Look for rain before the night.

Onion: Onion skins very thin,
Midwinter coming in,
Onion skins very tough,
Winter's coming cold and rough.

Pig: When pigs carry sticks, the clouds
will play tricks;
When they lie in the mud, no fears of
a flood.

Rainbow: Rainbow in the eastern sky,
The morrow will be dry;
Rainbow in the west that gleams,
Rain falls in streams.

Rooster: If the cock crows going to bed,
He will certainly rise with a watery head.

Sea gull: Sea gull, sea gull, sit on the
sand,
It's never good weather while you're on
the land.

Sheep: When sheep do huddle by tree
and bush,
Bad weather is coming with wind and
slush.

Snail: When black snails on the road
you see,
Then on the morrow rain will be.

Snow: Year of snow,
Crops will grow.

Spider: When spiders weave their webs
by noon,
Fine weather is coming soon.

Swallow: Swallows fly high: clear
blue sky;
Swallows fly low: rain we shall know.

Trout: When trout refuse bait or fly,
There ever is a storm a-nigh.

Candlemas Day (February 2): If
Candlemas Day be fine and clear,
We shall have winter half the year.

St. Romanus' Day (February 28): St.
Romanus bright and clear,
Augurs a goodly year.

St. Vitus' Day (June 15): If St. Vitus'
Day be rainy weather,
It will rain for thirty days together.

St. Swithin's Day (July 15): St.
Swithin's Day, if ye do rain,
For forty days it will remain.

St. Matthew's Day (September 22):
Matthew's Day bright and clear,
Brings good wine in next year.

Lent: Dry Lent, fertile year.

Good Friday: A wet Good Friday, very
little hay.
    In Albert Lee, *Weather Wisdom,* 1976

Looking at Weather in the Early United States

Americans from Benjamin Franklin to Smithsonian Institution scientists studied —and tried to predict—the weather long before satellites and computers came on the scene.

Franklin's Legacy

Early America's greatest generalist was interested in the nature of storms, not just lightning.

Benjamin Franklin's investigations of the electrical nature of lightning, although well known, were only one aspect of his broad interests in geophysical phenomena. Franklin formulated hypotheses on the role of electricity in causing precipitation and auroral phenomena and on the role of moist, heated air in causing waterspouts, whirlwinds, thunderstorms, and the equator-to-pole atmospheric circulation. Franklin also provided a conduit to America for European scientific opinion and philosophical instruments. His speculations on the role of electricity, heat, and the whirling motion of the winds provide the backdrop for the theories of succeeding generations of American meteorologists.

One of Franklin's many interests was comparing meteorological observations from different locales. Writing to Jared Eliot in Connecticut in 1747, Franklin thought it both advantageous and interesting to know the weather from "the several parts of the Country." He noted that storms along the coast sometimes persisted for three or four days and moved from the southwest toward the northeast even though the wind blew from the northeast. Franklin's deduction came from his attempt, in 1743, to observe an eclipse of the moon in Philadelphia. Storm clouds blowing in from the northeast obscured the view, but the eclipse was observed in Boston as scheduled; the storm arrived there four hours after it was noticed in Philadelphia. By collecting reports of the weather from travelers and compiling newspaper accounts from New England to Georgia, he concluded that storms with winds from the northeast began in the southwest, in Georgia or the Carolinas, and traveled toward the northeast at a rate of one hundred miles per hour.

Franklin gave two analogies to explain the cause of these storms. The first was the motion of water in a long canal when a gate is suddenly opened. All the water moves toward the gate, but there is a successive delay in the time when motion begins. The water nearest the gate begins to move first, causing progressive motion of the water in the length of the canal. The water at the head of the canal is the last to move. A second example supposed the air in a room to be at rest until a fire is set in the chimney. The heated air in the chimney rises immediately, and the air flows toward the chimney, and so on to the back of the room. Thus Franklin's hypothesis to explain northeast storms supposed "some great heat and rarefaction of the air in or about the Gulph of Mexico," which caused the air to rise and be replaced by a successive current of cooler, denser air from the north. The strike of the coast and the ridge of the Appalachian Mountains guided the northeast flow of air.

Weather Telegraphy

The earliest weather forecast in the United States was made possible by the cooperation of many telegraph operators in the eastern part of the country.

From the earliest experiments in the late 1840s to the creation of a federal storm-warning service under the U.S. Army Signal Office in 1870, telegraphy was the premier new technology of the meteorological community.... After the Civil War, Cleveland Abbe began issuing water reports and forecasts from the Cincinnati Observatory. Abbe's colleague Increase A. Lapham was convinced that the nation needed a federal telegraphic storm-warning system and successfully petitioned Congress to pass the enabling legislation. Although telegraphy was a marvelous new tool that increased the speed of reporting many times over and provided meteorologists with information on current weather conditions over a large area, it also produced an important shift of emphasis in meteorology from weather science to weather service. The efficiency of a network in bringing timely and accurate warnings to the public took priority over more theoretical concerns.

In the wake of Samuel F. B. Morse's federally funded telegraphic experiment between Washington and Baltimore in 1844 and the rapid expansion of lines to Philadelphia, New York, and Boston the following year, American meteorologists' dreams of instantaneous communication of weather data between cities gave way to practical arrangements that would make it a reality. Redfield's opinion, published in 1846, was the first to appear in print: "In the Atlantic ports, the approach of a gale may be made known by means of the electric telegraph, which probably will soon extend from Maine to the Mississippi." Loomis, in his "Report on the Meteorology of the United States," included suggestions for making the telegraph "subservient" to the protection of commerce from the ravages of storms. Henry intended to employ telegraphy in scientific studies at the Smithsonian.

The first daily weather reports were compiled from information sent, not by telegraph, but by trains. James Glaisher, secretary of the British Meteorological Society, arranged for observations to be taken each morning at 9:00 AM at railway stations, the results to be transported to London for publication the following day. These day-old observations first appeared in tabular form in the *London Daily News* for June 14, 1849. Glaisher also prepared surface weather maps from the data. Two years later, between August 8 and October 11, 1851, the Electric Telegraph Company provided experimental telegraphic weather reports to the Crystal Palace Exhibition. Daily maps, prepared from data, were put on display.

Concurrent with these developments in England, Henry was planning to "establish observations along the line of the telegraph, and to make observations on the origin and progress of storms." By the end of June 1849, Henry had petitioned the telegraph companies for the use of their lines for meteorological purposes. Henry O'Reilly, who along with Amos Kendall and Morse was constructing a telegraph line from Pennsylvania to St. Louis, promised that "Every necessary facility" would be afforded by his company free of costs. Similar promises were received from managers of the northern and southern lines. At the Smithsonian, Edward Foreman constructed a large map of the United States, in hopes of displaying the telegraphic reports, and Henry wrote to Glaisher at the Greenwich "Meteorological observatory" for information about procedures and forms used in the British railway system. There is no evidence, however, that a report or map was prepared until 1856. Scattered telegrams were received but not in sufficient numbers to prepare a general picture of the nation's weather. Nevertheless, some early reports were received by telegraph.

Alexander Jones, a reporter for the Associated Press in New York, was a pioneer in organizing cooperative press services and marketing wire reports among American cities. Known for having filed the first news message by telegraph from New York to Washington in 1846, Jones now attempted to begin a commercial system of telegraphic weather reports. On behalf of "Jones and Company," he advertised his services in the *American Journal of Science* in 1848, offering "colleges, universities, and other public institutions" daily meteorological reports from around the country on the "most reasonable terms of 12 1/2 to 25 cents per day per report for each city." Hoping that the government or the Smithsonian might assist his endeavor by supplying telegraph stations with meteorological instruments, he wrote to Henry: "By the way of experiment I obtained the enclosed observations yesterday and the day before, over a large tract up country in this state, which though not as complete as such observations ought to be, yet they are interesting. I am induced to believe that if the Government or the Regents of the Smithsonian Institute were to supply every Telegraph Station in the United States with suitable instruments,…correct and extensive observations might be simultaneously obtained over the greater part of the United States, by which the progress of storms could be accurately noted, and their course duly ascertained."

Although Jones was quite aggressive, sending weather information to help make up the circuits each morning was a routine habit, if not a duty, of many operators. Abbe received the following testimony from an early operator, David Brooks: "About the year 1849 I became manager in Philadelphia, and was in the habit of getting information about the condition of the lines westward every morning. If I learned from Cincinnati that the wires to St. Louis were interrupted by rain, I was tolerably sure a 'northeast' storm was approaching (from the west or southwest). For cold waves we looked in Chicago."....

Captain Joseph Brooks, manager of a line of steamers between Portland and Boston, recalled that in 1849 he received three telegraphic reports daily, morning, noon, and evening, from New York, Albany, and Plattsburgh: "'If the weather looked bad in the morning, the agent in New York was to send a dispatch at 8 o'clock; if a storm came up, to send another about noon; and then at 3 o'clock to give a full statement of its condition.' With these data Captain Brooks could tell when the storm would reach New Haven, Springfield, Boston, Portland, and other points. If the storm had been raging with severity in New York for some hours he knew it would not be safe for the Portland boat to leave."... By 1848 there were 2,100 wire miles; by 1850, 12,000 wire miles; and by 1852, 23,000 wire miles in service.

In 1856 the Smithsonian began to display the telegraphic weather messages it received on a large map of the United States which hung in the great hall of the institution. A piece of iron wire was driven into the map at each point of observation, and colored circular cards of about an inch in diameter were hung on the wires to indicate the weather and wind direction. White represented fair weather, blue indicated snow, black meant rain, and brown, cloudiness. Each card had an arrow painted on it and eight holes punched around the circumference so that the card could be hung to indicate the direction of the prevailing winds. Reports were received about ten o'clock each morning and were changed as often as new information was received. Special weather flags were also flown from the high tower of the Smithsonian building to indicate forthcoming weather conditions, especially on nights when Smithsonian lectures were scheduled. One May 1, 1857, the *Washington Evening Star* first published a report of the current weather at nineteen telegraph stations, all near the eastern seaboard on the line from New York to New Orleans. A week later, on May 7, the *Evening Star* published the first weather forecast in America, probably prepared by Henry and Espy: "Yesterday there was a severe storm south of Macon, Ga.; but from the fact that it is still clear this morning at that place and at Wheeling, it is *probable* that the storm was of a local character." These telegraphic investigations served the dual purpose of exciting public interest in meteorology and confirming Espy's earlier inferences on the eastward propagation of storms, "that as a general rule the storms of our latitude pursue a definite course."

James Rodger Fleming
Meteorology in America, 1800–1870, 1990

The International Meteorological Community

A quick look at the birth and early development of weather services in the United States and Europe.

Simple compilations of the various dates of the founding of national weather services in the nineteenth century…do not reveal the complex texture of events in this predisciplinary era of science. The result [is] a rather inaccurate and misleading chronology …which indicated that developments in the United States trailed those in Europe and Russia by several decades. The result is vastly different when meteorological systems, rather than weather services, are made the basis for comparison.

Belgium

Regular observations of pressure, temperature, and humidity were begun at the Brussels Observatory on January 1, 1833.… Construction of the observatory began in 1827, but as a result of the revolution of 1840, the observatory established by the Dutch regime was deprived of its astronomical instruments. [Director] Quetelet therefore emphasized meteorological research. Special observations were made on solar radiation, the soil temperature at different depths, and the periodic phenomena of plants. Because of the small size of the country and the relative uniformity of its climate, the establishment of a meteorological network was not of primary importance. A weather service was eventually established in 1878 by Quetelet's successor, Jean Houzeau, and consisted of only three weather stations and thirty climatological stations.

Germany

Until the 1870s, systems of meteorological observation in the German states suffered from the political fragmentation of the region. Nevertheless, inspired by the early example of Mannheim, numerous Germanic unions were attempted....

The Prussian Meteorological Institute was established in October 1847 in Berlin with Carl H. W. Mahlman...as director. In 1848 its scope was roughly comparable to the early Smithsonian meteorological project: there were thirty-five stations, a staff consisting of two persons, and a budget of 9,000 marks (approximately $3,000).... Bavaria organized a meteorological network centered in Munich in 1878. Small networks were also established in Baden, Württemberg, and Saxony.

England

Until 1823 there was no meteorological society or association in England. Long series of individual records were kept, but there was no uniformity of combined effort in observation. The Meteorological Society of London, founded in 1823, set no higher standards. Members needed no qualification other "than a desire to promote the science of Meteorology." The group soon sank into quiescence "from a want of zeal."

The society was revived in 1836 and produced the first English rainfall map in 1840 with results from fifty-two stations. In the first volume of its *Transactions* (1839), John Ruskin of Oxford set out the ambitious goals of the society: "The Meteorological Society...has been formed, not for a city, nor for a kingdom, but for the world. It wishes to be the central point, the moving power, of a vast machine, and it feels that unless it can be this, it must be powerless; if it

cannot do all, it can do nothing." But the Meteorological Society of London held meetings for only three more years and ceased its publications soon thereafter. Results from this group of enthusiasts were far from trustworthy. As George Symons noted in his history of English meteorological societies, "I have seen results published as air temperatures obtained from thermometers inside a hen house, I have seen a rain gauge under the eaves of a cottage, and another under a tree."

In 1850 the British Meteorological Society was founded to establish a "general system of observation, uniformity of registry, systematic communication, and other measures for insuring precision to the advancement of the aerostatical branch of physics." James Glaisher was elected secretary and organized the first current daily weather reports from reports sent by train along lines running to London. A royal charter was granted to the Meteorological Society in 1866.

In 1854 the British Board of Trade established a Meteorological Department with Robert Fitzroy, former captain of the *Beagle*, as director; he served until 1865. Fitzroy coordinated observations, reports, and the compilation of data but issued no forecasts. It was not until 1859, when 457 people died in the wreck of the luxury ship *Royal Charter* during a storm off the coast of Wales, that Fitzroy set up a coastal warning system in Britain. The network included fifteen stations in Britain and additional reports from Paris. Fitzroy's budget was £2,989. The Meteorological office was established in 1867, but the British Meteorological Council did not produce a daily weather map until 1872. The budget for meteorology was £4,500 ($21,000) in 1874....

France

In 1854 Le Verrier replaced Arago as director of the Paris Observatory. The same year a destructive gale in the Crimean Sea near the port of Balaklava wrecked Anglo-French transport ships during the Crimean War. In response, the observatory began an experiment in telegraphing weather facts. It did not, however, issue warnings. It was not until 1863 that Le Verrier telegraphed forecasts of impending weather. That was largely because the Paris Observatory was limited to its own observations. Although there were many observers in France, there was no central organization. The first notable government organization began in 1864, when Le Verrier, with the approval of the minister of public instruction, invited the councils-general to establish observing stations at normal schools in France. Fifty-eight schools responded. In addition, various departmental commissions collected observations made under their control and forwarded them to the Paris Observatory. In addition to the observers, clergy, medical men, teachers, and others maintained a meteorological correspondence. Most, however, observed without instruments. One of the products of this joint venture was the *Atlas météorologique de la France* (1865–76), which presented, among other things, a study of thunderstorms. Another series, *Nouvelles météorologiques* (1868–76), contained detailed observations from approximately sixty stations, but the stations were not inspected or standardized until 1873. It was not until after the death of Le Verrier in 1877 that the Bureau Central Météorologique de France was founded. Its director was Eleuthère Mascart, and its budget in 1878 was about $12,000.

Russia

Before 1835, Russia had only a few widely scattered private meteorological observers. Because of the Magnetische Verein, eight magnetic observatories were set up in Russia. By 1837 A. Ya. Kupffer had established meteorological stations at seven locations run by the Institute of Mining Engineers and at four other observatories....

The Central Physical Observatory published its observations separately in the *Annales de l'observatoire physique central* (1849–64). By 1849, the observatory was sponsoring a meteorological project roughly comparable to that of the Smithsonian. The staff of six had a budget of 9,000 rubles (about $7,000), and received data from eight principal stations (hourly observations) and forty-eight private observers (monthly journals). The number of private observers declined to twenty-four by 1864. Moreover, they had no standard instruments, methods, or times of observation.... The director of the observatory, Kupffer, was also in charge of the department of standard weights and measures for the Russian Empire. He established the first Russian telegraphic weather reports in 1864, but this network was limited to nine inland and two foreign stations, and no particular use was made of the reports....

Heinrich Wild, director from 1868

FOUNDING OF WEATHER SERVICES

1826	Belgium	Observatoire Royal
1847	Germany	Meteorologische Institut Berlin
1849	Russia	Central Physical Observatory
1854	Great Britain	Meteorological Department of the Board of Trade
1855	France	Observatoire
1870	United States	Weather Bureau (Signal Service)

to 1895, was trained in Switzerland, where he had been in charge of the Swiss meteorological stations and had established standardized instruments and procedures. When he came to Russia he found numerous errors in the observations and was surprised that none of the meteorological stations had been inspected for the past twenty years. Wild brought a new standard of observation to the Russian Empire. … In 1872, with the cooperation of the Hydrographic Department, Wild began a lithographed meteorological bulletin which contained telegraphic reports from fifty-five stations (thirty-six in Russia and nineteen in Europe and Asia) and provided synoptic charts for Russia and parts of Asia. Telegraphic storm warnings commenced in 1874.…

United States

The development of meteorological systems in the United States did not lag behind Europe and Russia and was indeed quite similar. The nineteenth-century era of expanding horizons was in fact an international phenomenon. Climatic surveys of various nations were widespread in the first half of the century, telegraphic experiments began in the 1850s, and storm warning services were established in the 1860s and 1870s. International cooperation soon followed.

Because of its well-funded weather service (over $400,000 in 1874), America soon took the lead in international cooperation in meteorology. General Myer, representing the United States at the Vienna conference of directors of weather services in 1873, proposed that the nations of the world prepare an international series of simultaneous observations to aid the study of world climatology and weather patterns. Myer's suggestion led to the *Bulletin of International Simultaneous Observations,* published by the signal office beginning in 1875. The *Bulletin* contained worldwide synoptic charts and summaries of observations recorded simultaneously at numerous locations around the world. The "metrological" standards established by the work of these international congresses initiated a new era of worldwide observation and more homogeneous data inscription as a practical result.

James Rodger Fleming
Meteorology in America, 1800–1870
1990

A Great American Weather Story

Every year the United States sees some of the world's most spectacular weather, from tornadoes and hurricanes to droughts and floods. But the Blizzard of 1888 has its own special place in history.

W*inter—Fifth Avenue* by Alfred Stieglitz captures the bleakness of a blizzard in New York City.

No storm that has ever visited the East has built such a legend for itself, nor any deserve to be remembered as well, as the Blizzard of 1888. Nearly 100 years have elapsed since the waning days of winter in March of 1888, long enough so that virtually no one living today could give a first-hand account of the storm, and yet it stands as the epitome of winter storms and probably always will. Each passing season brings unusually heavy snows to some portion of the country, and the cold winds still sweep across the arctic tundra, plunging temperatures to new lows, but rarely do the forces of snow, wind, and penetrating cold combine to produce such results over so large an area as the famed Blizzard of 1888.

The meteorological circumstances of the storm are in themselves quite interesting. Springlike weather had asserted itself throughout much of the East, sending temperatures well into the forties and fifties over several days preceding the storm. In fact, forecasters had predicted gentle southeast wind with rain arriving only a day before the event that most contemporary meteorologists would rather forget. A storm was crossing the Great Lakes, dragging with it bitterly cold weather on its western flanks. Meanwhile, another disturbance was taking shape in the southeastern states, destined, the prophets felt, to bring rain due to the mild temperatures that the East was experiencing. With twenty-twenty hindsight, it is easy to illustrate how they underestimated the impact of the cold front that was charging through the Midwest. That cold air interacted with the developing storm in the South, energizing that system. The consequences were disastrous.

As the storm moved slowly northward, light rain broke out in the middle Atlantic states, and the rain grew heavier as the temperatures in D.C. fell from the fifties to the thirties. Gradually, snow and hail began to mix into the precipitation pattern, and telegraph and telephone wires began to snap. At sundown, on Sunday, March 11, temperatures in the Mid-Atlantic skidded to freezing and the snow began to accumulate. Further north, New York City was experiencing torrential rains, which fell in sheets flooding the streets, as temperatures eased back from the low forties. By midnight, the precipitation there, too, was changing to snow, but few were aware of the incredible sight they were to face the following morning. They might just as well have stayed in bed. Overnight, temperatures slipped through the twenties and the wind shifted to the northwest, howling through the chimneys of the sleeping towns. Later the next day, in the raging storm, conditions worsened while the temperature plummeted to only five above. One can scarcely imagine the additional accumulation of snow had all the precipitation of the previous day been frozen....

A woman was seen wading through a gigantic drift [on Monday], struggling every step of the way, and only halfway through, seemingly overcome with exhaustion, she fell flat in the drift. About half a dozen men who had witnessed her plight came to her aid, and before she could be reached, the fierce wind had completely covered her with snow. The body of a twelve-year-old newsboy was discovered three days later in the snow near Fulton Avenue in New York, frozen to death. While he was not immediately identified, his name was presumed to be Fischer, for he had not been heard from since leaving home on Monday.

Many others, fortunately, found the elements too overwhelming and returned home to spend the day with their families by the fire. The New York Times observed how difficult it must have been for "good steady church-going heads of families when they had to get through breakfast without their favorite newspaper, their hot buttered rolls and their fragrant coffee enriched with boiling milk." They began to question "whether life was worth living at all, with all these trials and tribulations to undergo."...

Tuesday morning dawned in an unprecedented spectacle of a snowfall that had lain untouched for the better part of thirty hours. Snow was piled, in some cases, to the second-storey windows, and people gradually began to tunnel out of their homes. It was not until Wednesday that the novelty wore off and most decided that it was time to do something about it. When the sidewalks were cleared, piles of snow along them were built up so high that one could not see across the street. Many men built caves in the big banks and built fires in them to melt the snow or turned streams of hot water upon the big heaps. Snow began anew Wednesday afternoon, and it was forecast to be a heavy fall, but it did not materialize. The snow changed to rain, and by sundown the sun peeked through the clouds. Overall, the situation was accepted with universal good nature, and one pile of snow, about fifteen feet high, bore a sign reading "This snow for sale." There were no takers.

Ti Sanders
The Weather Is Front Page News, 1983

Lewis Fry Richardson's Pioneering Fantasy

While World War I raged, an English meteorologist serving with a British ambulance unit pondered Vilhelm Bjerknes' theories about applying numerical calculation to weather prediction. Part theater, part factory, the computing center he envisioned borders on science fiction. This text was originally published in Weather Prediction by Numerical Process, *1922.*

Lewis Fry Richardson's research in weather forecast calculation (1913–6) was interrupted by a two-year stint in the Friends' Ambulance Unit (1916–8). To the regret of many of his colleagues, he left the Meteorological Office when it was incorporated into the Air Ministry (1920) because of his pacifist convictions.

It took me the best part of six weeks to draw up the computing forms and to work out the new distribution in two vertical columns for the first time. My office was a heap of hay in a cold rest billet. With practice the work of an average computer might go perhaps ten times faster. If the time-step were 3 hours, then 32 individuals could just compute two points so as to keep pace with the weather, if we allow nothing for the very great gain in speed which is invariably noticed when a complicated operation is divided up into simpler parts, upon which individuals specialize. If the coordinate chequer were 200 km square in plan, there would be 3200 columns on the complete map of the globe. In the tropics the weather is often foreknown, so that we may say 2000 active columns. So that 32 x 2000 = 64,000 computers would be needed to trace the weather for the whole globe. That is a staggering figure. Perhaps in some years' time it may be possible to report a simplification of the process. But in any case, the organization indicated is a central forecast-factory for the whole globe, or for portions extending to boundaries where the weather is steady, with individual computers specializing on the separate equations. Let us hope for their sakes that they are moved on from time to time to new operations.

After so much hard reasoning, may one play with a fantasy? Imagine a large hall like a theatre, except that the circles and galleries go right round through the space usually occupied by the stage. The walls of this chamber are painted to form a map of the globe. The ceiling represents the north polar regions, England is in the gallery, the tropics in the upper circle, Australia on the dress circle, and the antarctic in the pit. Myriad computers are at work upon the weather of the part of the map where each sits, but each computer attends only to one equation or part of an equation. The work of each region is coordinated by an official of higher rank. Numerous little "night signs" display the instantaneous values so that neighbouring computers can read them. Each number is thus displayed in three adjacent zones so as to maintain communication to the North and South on the map. From the floor of the pit a tall pillar rises to half the height of the hall. It carries a large pulpit on its top. In this sits the man in charge of the whole theatre; he is surrounded by several assistants and messengers. One of his duties is to maintain a uniform speed of progress in all parts of the globe. In this respect he is like the conductor of an orchestra in which the instruments are slide-rules and calculating machines. But instead of waving a baton he turns a beam of rosy light upon any region that is running ahead of the rest, and a beam of blue light upon those who are behindhand.

Four senior clerks in the central pulpit are collecting the future weather as fast as it is being computed and despatching it by pneumatic carrier to a quiet room. There it will be coded and telephoned to the radio transmitting station.

Messengers carry piles of used computing forms down to a storehouse in the cellar.

In a neighbouring building there is a research department, where they invent improvements. But there is much experimenting on a small scale before any change is made in the complex routine of the computing theatre. In a basement an enthusiast is observing eddies in the liquid lining of a huge spinning bowl, but so far the arithmetic proves the better way. In another building are all the usual financial, correspondence, and administrative offices. Outside are playing fields, houses, mountains and lakes, for it was thought that those who compute the weather should breathe of it freely.

In Oliver M. Ashford,
Prophet or Professor: The Life and Work of Lewis Fry Richardson,
1985

The Power of Clouds

It had always been thought that clouds were more passive indicators of short-term weather than driving forces of long-term climate. Researchers are now beginning to appreciate the degree to which clouds determine how much sunlight the Earth accepts or rejects and how much heat it yields back to space. Groups like the Center for Clouds, Chemistry, and Climate (known as C^4) in La Jolla, California, a consortium of university, government, and industrial researchers in the United States and Europe, are now trying to uncover the radiative effects of clouds.

The sunlight that gets through the cloud cover warms Earth's surface, and this heat must eventually be shed. The planet gets rid of it in two ways. Some it radiates directly in the form of infrared energy.... This energy keeps getting absorbed and reradiated close to Earth's surface, raising the temperature and thus creating the greenhouse effect that enables life to be maintained here....

The other way the planet cools itself is by releasing "latent" heat. When a water molecule jumps from liquid to vapor form, it sucks in energy from its surroundings.... Latent heat has long been credited with being the driving force behind worldwide weather patterns. The theory starts with the observation that incoming sunlight is not distributed uniformly across Earth's surface—the tropics receive about two and a half times more energy than do the poles. As water evaporates from the tropics, rises through the atmosphere, and releases its heat, a lot of energy is injected into the higher altitudes. Latent heat kick-starts a global engine that attempts to bring the planet into equilibrium by moving warm air toward the cold poles. As the air cools and sinks down to the spinning Earth, the complexities of our weather are created....

The theory makes for a tidy climatic story, one in which clouds don't count for much. They are incidental by-products of latent heat, mere ornamentation on the weather engine. The only problem with the story, as the researchers at C^4 are discovering, is that the numbers won't support the plot.

For [C^4's director, Veerabhadran] Ramanathan, and many of his colleagues, clouds are a relatively new passion. Twenty years ago most of them were just starting to wonder whether the carbon dioxide and other gases generated by burning fossil fuels might amplify the natural greenhouse effect and threaten to overheat the planet. Ramanathan, for example, was the first to calculate that the ozone-destroying chlorofluorocarbons were also powerful greenhouse gases. But in the mid-1980s, though, he realized how limited his information was. "After ten years of writing papers," says Ramanathan, "It became clear that almost anything I had to say about climate change was probably not worth much, because I couldn't tell how the clouds were going to respond."

Increasing the amount of carbon dioxide in the air, computer models suggest, should increase the temperature. Warmer air will also hold more water vapor, which could increase the greenhouse effect by as much as 50 percent. All told, a doubling of CO_2 might heat the planet by 3 to 8 degrees. It's also possible, though, that a warmer, moister atmosphere would create a different pattern of cloud cover, which might dramatically enhance the heating or counteract it. But in the early 1980s, climatologists couldn't say what the normal net effect of clouds was, much less predict what clouds would do in the future.

Ramanathan devised a way to get some answers. At the time, NASA was designing three satellites known collectively as the Earth Radiation Budget Experiment (ERBE) to monitor the planet's incoming and outgoing heat. By fiddling with the satellite findings, Ramanathan realized, he could estimate the radiative effect of clouds. First he needed to identify the clear sky in ERBE's data. From space,

cloudless regions would show up as the darkest (since they would reflect less sunshine back at the satellite) and would release the most heat (since they couldn't block escaping infrared radiation). Also, without a patchwork of clouds on top of them, the clear areas would look much more uniform. Once he had identified the clear regions, he could subtract them out of ERBE's data and be left with nothing but clouds.

It was not a simple calculation. Although the satellite launches began in 1984, not until 1989 were Ramanathan and six colleagues able to announce their verdict. For now, they said, clouds cool the planet more effectively than they heat it, removing the heat of a 60-watt lightbulb from every six-by-six-foot patch of Earth's surface. This was a huge amount of radiation to block;

Altocumulus clouds.

the results showed that at present, net cloud cooling is four times greater than the warming expected from doubling CO_2. Without clouds, the planet could be 20 degrees hotter....

The ERBE scanners, designed only to record radiation, could not tell Ramanathan what kinds of clouds he was dealing with. He and his coworkers had to rely on ship observations of prevailing cloud types in each region. Once they paired the Earth-based observations with the satellite derived data, they found that different types of clouds reflected sunlight and absorbed rising heat differently. Bright banks of stratus clouds form vast tracks over the North Atlantic and North Pacific and also blanket the Southern Ocean around Antarctica; these are far better reflectors than absorbers and produce

Winslow Homer's 1891 *The Woodcutter* (detail), a study of clouds.

the most net cooling. In contrast, the high cirrus ice clouds of the tropics absorb enough heat to cancel out their reflective cooling.

The distribution of these cloud effects—more warming in the tropics than in the mid to high latitudes—is as important as latent heat in creating the atmospheric temperature gradient that drives the tropical heat engine. David Randall, an atmospheric scientist at Colorado State University, compared a climate model that contained cloud effects with one without them. Without the clouds, there was simply not enough heat to distribute to the poles, and so weather patterns slowed down dramatically. Also crucial was the correct position of the clouds. If they were scattered randomly, the models acted bizarrely: the oceans tried to transport their own heat backward from the poles to the equator to compensate for the misplaced clouds.

"Latent heat is still important," says Randall. "It's just that we used to think it was an 800-pound gorilla and now it's a 500-pound gorilla." That extra weight has gone to clouds....

[Additional research indicates that clouds may actually even absorb a substantial amount of energy.] Not everyone accepts these conclusions. A healthy skepticism remains, says Ramanathan, because no one can yet explain how clouds can absorb so much sunlight. Some suggest it's the work of the cloud's droplets or ice crystals; others believe it's due to pollutants or natural impurities they carry. Perhaps photons jostle their way among the cloud particles or bounce back and forth between patchy clouds. "Maybe there's something going on in the phase shift from vapor to liquid water or ice

Homer's *Eight Bells* also illuminates the painter's fascination with weather.

that we don't understand," Robert Cess [of the State University of New York at Stony Brook] acknowledges.

Whatever the mechanism at work, though, researchers realized that if their measurements were right, clouds must be even more critical to driving the global heat engine than they thought. With sunlight being absorbed in clouds, the atmosphere needs even less latent heating from the ground to put the circulation patterns in motion. Modelers are just now beginning to incorporate these latest results into their simulations. Eventually they should be able to build models that accurately predict how clouds will behave in an atmosphere altered by humanity, and how the climate will act in response. But first they will have to learn a lot more about how the physics and chemistry of clouds affect their radiative properties.

"The ultimate solution," says Ramanathan, "will come when we can have beautiful cloud pictures on the wall and know their radiative properties just by looking at them." For now they must keep their gaze focused on the hard numbers. "None of us," Ramanathan adds, "are ready for real clouds yet."

Yvonne Baskin
"Under the Influence of Clouds"
Discover, September 1995

Further Reading

BOOKS

Calder, Nigel, *The Weather Machine*, Viking Press, New York, 1974

Carpenter, Clive, *The Changing World of Weather*, Facts on File, New York, 1991

Day, John A., and Vincent Schaefer, *Peterson's Field Guides: Clouds and Weather*, Houghton Mifflin, Boston, 1991

Demillo, Rob, *How Weather Works*, Ziff-Davis Press, Emeryville, California, 1994

Dunlop, Storm, and Francis Wilson, *Macmillan Field Guides: Weather and Forecasting*, Macmillan, New York, 1987

Fleming, James Rodger, *Meteorology in America, 1800–1870*, Johns Hopkins University Press, Baltimore, 1990

Frier, George D., *Weather Proverbs: How 600 Proverbs, Sayings and Poems Accurately Explain Our Weather*, Fisher Books, Tucson, 1989

Frisinger, H. Howard, *The History of Meteorology: to 1800*, Science History Publications, New York, 1977

Gleick, James, *Chaos: Making a New Science*, Viking Press, New York, 1987

Gribbin, John, *What's Wrong With Our Weather? The Climatic Threat of the 21st Century*, Scribner's, New York, 1979

Halacy, D. S., Jr., *The Weather Changers*, Harper and Row, New York, 1968

Hardy, Ralph, Peter Wright, John Kingston, and John Gribben, *The Weather Book*, Little Brown, 1982

Ladurie, Emmanuel Le Roy, *Times of Feast, Times of Famine: The History of Climate Since the Year 1000*, trans. Barbara Bray, Doubleday, Garden City, New York, 1971

Lee, Albert, *Weather Wisdom*, Doubleday, Garden City, New York, 1976

Lockhart, Gary, *The Weather Companion*, John Wiley and Sons, New York, 1988

Middleton, W. E. Knowles, *Invention of the Meteorological Instruments*, Johns Hopkins University Press, Baltimore, 1969

Posey, Carl A., *The Living Earth Book of Wind and Weather*, Reader's Digest, Pleasantville, New York, 1994

Revkin, Andrew, *Global Warming: Understanding the Forecast*, Abbeville Press, New York, 1992

Sanders, Ti, *The Weather Is Front Page News*, Icarus Press, South Bend, Indiana, 1983

Schneider, Stephen H., *Global Warming: Are We Entering the Greenhouse Century?*, Sierra Club Books, San Francisco, 1989

Wagner, Ronald L., and Bill Adler, Jr., *The Weather Sourcebook*, Globe Pequot Press, Old Saybrook, Connecticut, 1994

Watson, Lyall, *Heaven's Breath: A Natural History of the Wind*, William Morrow, New York, 1984

Williams, Jack, *The Weather Book*, Random House, New York, 1992

MAGAZINES

For information on *Weatherwise*, the only popular weather magazine in the United States, write to: 1319 18th St., N.W., Washington, DC 20036; or call 202-296-6267.

Metric Conversions

DISTANCE		TEMPERATURE	
	1 kilometer = .62 miles		$(°F - 32) \times 5/9 = °C$
	1 meter = 39.37 inches		$°C \times 9/5 + 32 = °F$
	1 cm = .39 inch		
	1 mile = 1.6 kilometers		
	1 foot = 30.48 centimeters		
	1 inch = 2.54 centimeters		

List of Illustrations

Index

Acknowledgments

The author and publishers wish to thank Météo-France for their cooperation and assistance. The author joins Editions Gallimard in thanking the European Space Agency for its photographs, Jean Le Ber of the European Space Operations Center (Darmstadt), and Météo-France. Special thanks to Mrs. Groma and Messrs. J. Damiens, Patrick Donguy, Claude Fons, Michel Hontarrède, Jean-Pierre Javelle, and André Lebeau.

Photograph Credits

Text Credits

René Chaboud is a meteorologist for Météo-France,
the French weather service. In 1977 he was
instrumental in revamping weather bulletin
format for public broadcast, and in 1987 he became
one of the first weather announcers on French radio.
He has been a forecaster at the Lyons regional weather
center since 1980 and has written numerous
French books and articles on meteorology.

Translated from the French by I. Mark Paris

For Harry N. Abrams, Inc.
Editor: Sharon AvRutick
Typographic Designer: Elissa Ichiyasu
Design Supervisor: Miko McGinty
Assistant Designer: Tina Thompson

Library of Congress Catalog Card Number: 95–079943

ISBN 0–8109–2878–7

The author and the publishers are grateful to Météo-France
for its close collaboration and would also like to extend a special thanks
to Mrs. Gore-Dalle, OMM, Geneva.

Copyright © 1994 Gallimard

English translation copyright © 1996 Harry N. Abrams, Inc., New York,
and Thames and Hudson Ltd., London

Published in 1996 by Harry N. Abrams, Inc., New York
A Times Mirror Company

Printed and bound in Italy by Editoriale Libraria, Trieste